The Olympic Games, Sports Law and Human Rights

This book explores the relationship between sports law, the Olympic Movement and human rights. Examining the historical legal roots of contemporary "Olympic law", including the ancient history of the Olympic Games and the legacy of Pierre de Coubertin, this book shines new light on one of the most important issues in world sport today.

Written by a practising lawyer with expertise in sports law, this book explains the core concepts underpinning Olympic law and offers in-depth analysis of the Olympic Charter, arguing that the Charter is a key legal instrument in the context of which the interplay between ethics, rights and the Olympics must be understood. The book also examines key contemporary issues at the nexus of sports law and human rights, including religious freedom and protests by athletes.

Offering a new interdisciplinary perspective on Olympic law, drawing on legal theory, history and contemporary social scientific studies in sport, this book is fascinating reading for any advanced student, researcher, policymaker or practitioner with an interest in sports law, the Olympic Games, mega-events or human rights.

Alexandre Miguel Mestre is Assistant Professor at the Autonomous University of Lisbon, Portugal, and a legal counsel at the law firm Abreu Advogados, working primarily in the areas of sports law and European Union law. He is an independent member of the UEFA Governance and Compliance Committee; a member of the Aquatics Integrity Unit – the adjudicatory body of the International Swimming Federation/World Aquatics – and a member of the Pierre de Coubertin International Committee. He was Secretary of State for Sport in Youth in Portugal.

Routledge Focus on Sport, Culture and Society

Routledge Focus on Sport, Culture and Society showcases the latest cutting-edge research in the sociology of sport and exercise. Concise in form (20,000–50,000 words) and published quickly (within three months), the books in this series represents an important channel through which authors can disseminate their research swiftly and make an impact on current debates. We welcome submissions on any topic within the socio-cultural study of sport and exercise, including but not limited to subjects such as gender, race, sexuality, disability, politics, the media, social theory, Olympic Studies, and the ethics and philosophy of sport. The series aims to be theoretically-informed, empirically-grounded and international in reach, and will include a diversity of methodological approaches.

Available in this series:

Sport and Social Media in Business and Society
Gashaw Abeza and Ryan King-White

Skateboarding and the Senses
Skills, Surfaces, and Spaces
Sander Hölsgens and Brian Glenney

Essentials of Cerebral Palsy Football
Edited by Iván Peña González, Raúl Reina Vaillo, and Manuel Moya Ramón

National Symbols at the Olympic Games
An Olympics Without Flags?
Jörg Krieger

The Olympic Games, Sports Law and Human Rights
Alexandre Miguel Mestre

For more information about this series, please visit: www.routledge.com/Routledge-Focus-on-Sport-Culture-and-Society/book-series/RFSCS

The Olympic Games, Sports Law and Human Rights

Alexandre Miguel Mestre

LONDON AND NEW YORK

Designed cover image: Routledge

First published 2025
by Routledge
4 Park Square, Milton Park, Abingdon, Oxon OX14 4RN

and by Routledge
605 Third Avenue, New York, NY 10158

Routledge is an imprint of the Taylor & Francis Group, an informa business

British Library Cataloguing-in-Publication Data
A catalogue record for this book is available from the British Library

ISBN: 978-1-032-94257-5 (hbk)
ISBN: 978-1-032-94261-2 (pbk)
ISBN: 978-1-003-56974-9 (ebk)

DOI: 10.4324/9781003569749

Typeset in Times New Roman
by Apex CoVantage, LLC

Contents

Part I

Olympism, Olympic Games and sports law

Figure 0.1

1 The ancient games in the genis of the modern sports legal system

Sport

According to the Porto Editora (Infopédia) Dictionary, sport is "*physical exercise done in a methodical way, either individually, or in a group, for various reasons (competition, recreation, therapy, etc)*". The Priberam Dictionary defines sport as the "*[r]egular conduct of an activity that involves bodily exercise, which is governed by certain rules, for leisure, for physical development, or to demonstrate agility, dexterity or strength (e.g. school sport; leisure sport; and competitive sport*)".[1] It is clear from both definitions that the practice of sport can have different objectives or contexts.

There is no definition of sport in the regulatory texts issued by national sports organisations. This is also true in the case of state legislation, for, unlike what happened in 2004, when the legislator imported the concept of sport enshrined in the European Charter on Sport into the Basic Law of Sport,[2] there is currently no legal definition of sport.

As far as private international sport bodies are concerned, the Olympic Charter, the Magna Charter of the Olympic Movement adopted by the International Olympic Committee (IOC), contains no definition of sport, likewise, the (current) GAISF – *Global Association of International Sports Federations* makes no attempt to define sport,[3] unlike the *Sport Accord*, which did.

The only definition of sport to be found in international legal instruments adopted by states is the Council of Europe, European Sports Charter, which is soft law,[4] that is, non-binding, legal instrument. This necessarily complicates our task, which is to identify a binding definition of sport in the law and its legal provisions.

According to Article 2(1) of the said Charter, sport is *"all forms of physical activity which, through casual or organised participation, are aimed at maintaining or improving physical fitness and mental well-being, forming social relationships or obtaining results in competition at all levels"*. The concept of sport therefore includes two major "*forms of physical activity*", one that seeks to "*improve physical fitness*" and another that seeks "*results in competition at all levels*". There are therefore two distinct poles, "areas", or

DOI: 10.4324/9781003569749-2

subcomponents of sport, which theory (i.e. essentially the theory of the sport sciences, which has an impact on the legal community[5]) has highlighted as distinguishing "physical activity" as such, from the concept of sport.

The non-consensual, but frankly majority view, starts by identifying activity, which is primarily, but not exclusively, physical,[6] spontaneous, informal and non-systematic. Such activity is individual, or collective, and takes place in the context of the recreation, or (active/physical) leisure of the person, more in an emotional context, and for the purpose of self-fulfilment, health and quality of life, in a context that involves more or less socialisation. At most, the individual seeks to overcome the limits of their body and/or mind, but without having a competitive agenda, and without the need to comply with preordained requirements of conduct.[7] This is physical activity such as stair climbing, jogging on riverbanks, walking fast, performance of individual gymnastic exercises, or fitness activities in a gym, or health club.

They also acknowledges the existence of sport as a phenomena that is rule governed (codified, based on specific rules that provide an a priori definition of the competitive framework), institutionalised (with specific institutions, bodies and organisations, such as national federations) which are often professionalised, in which the body is exercised, most commonly in a group context, in which athletes compete with each other to achieve the best result, and to see who is best. This type of sport is competitive, based on competition with other competitors in order to see who is best (the champion), or to achieve the best result (the record). The competitors' aim is to maximise their performance. We refer to the sport within the associative movement, which includes clubs, associations, sports federations and Olympic and Paralympic Committees. At a more selective and higher level, this sport also includes high performance sport and the national teams. This level of competitive sport includes mass sport and professional sport, which is generally very exacting (i.e. limited to certain age groups and with non-ludic objectives), which distinguishes competitive sport from "sport for all" [eminently recreational, educational, leisure-related and socially inclusive, and can be engaged in throughout a lifetime, although with some age-related adaptations.]

Intermediate activities such as sport in school, either as part of the school curriculum, that is, physical education, or as an extracurricular activity, that is, school sport, are also included in the concept of sport.

It follows from the foregoing observations that sport is a polysemic concept that encapsulates multiple realities, which, in line with the Council of Europe definition, vary according to their objective, that is, the reason the individual takes part in the activity in question. It is therefore obvious that circumstances in which someone, who is not interested in being better than anyone else, occupies their free time in physical activity, differ from circumstances in which an individual, acting within a regulated, competitive, organised and/or institutionalised, and possibly professionalised, framework, seeks to win and be better than one, or more, opponents. However, and notwithstanding that difference, these two situations have something in common, to the extent that they both involve the same reality, that is, sport. And whatever the reason for the activity, it will nevertheless always be a sport. Likewise, it makes no fundamental difference whether the activity is organised or unorganised. However, what does make a difference in terms of the Council of Europe definition is the nature of the activity, as the concept of sport includes "*all forms of physical activity*".

The concept of sport is therefore very broad in legal terms and includes the concept of physical activity. However, we are of course aware that this opinion is far from consensual. In any event, this chapter focuses on the Olympic Games, which is a competition regarding which there is virtually no doubt that its subject matter is sport, and it is on the basis of this premise that we will now identify another concept, that is, the concept of Sports Law.

Sport law

Sport is a major social phenomenon, via which Humankind expresses its condition as an eminently social being that exerts its body and mind simultaneously. Furthermore, as law is concerned with any behaviour of Humankind in its social life, by ordering and disciplining that social life with rules and norms of conduct (compliance with which is ensured coercively via the imposition of penalties), it is completely natural that sport and Law are not indifferent to each other.

Eduardo GAMERO CASADO[8] defines this better when he states that sport is not only a legal concept but also a subject matter of Law. This Spanish author bases his view on the relevant legal theory and states, regarding sport in its competitive form, that law plays a founding role in sport, as sport cannot exist without rules, that sport activity is a legal and rule-governed world. Likewise, another well-known Spanish jurist, Gabriel REAL FERRER,[9] even argues that sport law was one of the first manifestations of law, precisely because sport is implicitly subject to certain rules. According to this author, it became necessary for sport to submit to law, that is, to a set of norms supported by the community, which include the corresponding penalties.

The founding role of rules in sports activity becomes more evident when competitive contexts are considered, in which the pre-existence of binding rules is necessary in order to have an agreed comparative and objective ranking of results. According to the best French legal theory,[10] the absence of rules would render the existence of the Law itself impossible. The central idea is as follows: the physical, technical, tactical and psychological aspects of sport in a competitive setting involve a struggle against time, or against an adversary (whether an individual or a team), which is inconceivable without the existence of rules. While it is true that these rules may be arbitrary – for example, the definition of a sprint as 100 metres, rather than 120 metres, or the choice of the size of a field of play as a certain size, rather than another, or a decision that a team must have 11 players, and not more, or less, than that, these rules must inevitably exist. This school of thought considers that the winning of a marathon or a long jump competition presupposes the existence of rules that govern the competition, which entrusts the integrity of the organisation of the event, for example, the fixing of a date, place, the attraction of competitors, to an entity, which is usually a sports federation.

Similarly, the Portuguese author, João LEAL AMADO,[11] clearly demonstrates that sport and law are inseparable. As we shall see from the following citation, the importance of this nexus lies precisely in the fact that the existence of a competition, bout or match results in a classification:

> *However, the truth is that the relationship between sport and law not only exists, but could not be closer, primarily because the very existence of sport (or rather competitive sport) invariably presupposes the existence of rules ("technical rules" and "rules of the game"). Indeed, anyone can run, or swim, or play with a ball, without the said activities being rule-governed; but no one can win a race, or compete in a game, without rules (e.g. rules that determine the distance to be run, or if the ball can be played with the hands, or the feet). Rules are an integral part of sport, rules are of the essence of sport, as only the existence of rules permits competition, and the identification of winners and losers. As JESTAZ comments, "au commencement était la règle: en sport, le règlement a un caractère fondateur". It can accordingly be stated that law creates sports activity, as the latter cannot exist without the former. There are those who consider that sport may even be the human activity in which law plays the greatest role.*

It is therefore undeniable that regardless of the greater or lesser connection between law and sport, the truth is that the pairing of law and sport not only exists but is inevitable, and gives rise to sport law. We can define sport law as a set, or complex, of written or customary norms, and specific principles that frame and govern the organisation and practice of sport, in its various forms. These rules are issued by private sports organisations (*particularly* sports federations) and by states, and their ambit of application can even be supranational or transnational.

There are various other possible definitions of sport law, two of which we consider to be very apt. The first is that of Luís Paulo RELÓGIO,[12] who defines sport law as an "*autonomous branch of the law, which is concerns the study of the norms that govern sports activity and the sport system, including a variety of sources of law, as sport law is not only concerned with law, but also with a wide range of hierarchically ranked areas, which govern innumerable aspects of the sport system and its actors, and also includes cooperative rules issued by the various institutions and regulatory bodies that have rule making competence regarding sport activity*". The second definition, which is proposed by Diogo FREITAS DO AMARAL,[13] provides a perfect synthesis:

sport law "[is] *the branch of law that comprises the system of international, national, public, private, state, and non-state legal norms that govern sports activities, and the control and supervision thereof by international private organisations and the state*".

According to history, the Olympic Games of Antiquity were the first true major sports competition of Humankind. As we have already seen, sport (essentially competitive sport) is inseparable from rules. Could the Olympic Games of Antiquity have existed without sport law? What effect did this sport law have on the modern sport legal system?

The sports legal system

The systematised legal norms of a particular community are its legal order, and its legal system. If we want to identify this community geographically, we can, for example, refer to the "Portuguese legal order". We believe that if we also want to view this legal framework in terms of subject matter, we can, for example, identify the "health legal order", the "environment legal order" and the "sport legal order".

We shall now concentrate, albeit only summarily, on the concept of the sport legal order, as this concept is far from being fully defined, despite the fact that it is frequently referred to.

In legal theory, J. Gomes CANOTILHO[14] makes a distinction between the "*sport legal* order" and the "*state legal order*", in which the former includes norms issued by sports organisations, and the latter is the "*state legal system*". Carlos FERREIRA DE ALMEIDA[15] opines similarly by breaking down "*sports (normative) frameworks*" into a "*sport order*" and "*state norms applicable* to sport", so that the former includes regulatory norms issued by private organisers of sport competitions, while the latter comprises state norms applicable to sport. In an annotation to the Sport Arbitration Court Law,[16] specifically Article 1(2) of Law 74/2013, of 6 September, he refers to "*disputes that arise regarding the sport legal order*", and conceives of the sport legal order as "*always including these public law norms, i.e. State norms, and the expression of these norms within the internal organisational regulation of sport by the sport federations*". Our view, as recently expressed elsewhere,[17] is that the sport legal order includes both public and private sources of law, and is basically the overarching order of all sport law, as defined earlier, that is, it includes all sources of law that are directly, or indirectly, linked with sport, whatever the legal nature of the body that adopts them.

In any case, for the purposes of this brief study, and having put aside the various currents of thought regarding this issue, as excellently described by Alexandra PESSANHA,[18] we shall essentially opt for the concept of a sport legal order developed by the Italian legal theorist GIANNINI, because we agree with her opinion that "*Giannini's thought is the most elaborate, and complete attempt to define the sports legal order in legal terms.*" This chain of thought, which is derived from SANTI ROMANO, amounts *"to the development of a theoretical construct, which, by highlighting the subjective, organisational, and regulatory aspects of sport, among others, stresses the fact that the sports community, like others, produces its own rules, has its own means to make and apply them, and an institutional unit with the power to decide disputes, and to punish offences committed in violation of the rules it has established".*

This theoretical construct will aid us in the development and conclusion of this brief study, and with the aspects that GIANNINI identified as the constitutive elements of a legal order, that is, (i) the existence of a multiplicity of natural, or juridical, persons; (ii) the existence of an autonomous organisational schema, that is, the idea of a system, that is, of an ordered, articulated, self-organised aggregation; (iii) the existence of a system of rules, of a common body of norms, a structured and coherent set of norms, with an overall logic and an internal developmental dynamic, to which the said multiplicity of persons regard as binding.

However, and with all due respect, we do not share GIANNINI's view, cited by Álvaro MELO FILHO,[19] that "*L'ordinamento dello sport rappresenta l'único caso di nascita e di formazione de un nuovo e complesso ordenamento giuridico nei tempi moderno*". We do not agree with GIANNINI because, as we will seek to demonstrate below, we consider that the Olympic Games of Antiquity were already governed by a true sport legal order, which was necessarily more incipient, than the current sport legal system, but which was already very similar to the contemporary sport legal order.

The inherently Greek Olympic Games of Antiquity obviously cannot be compared with the Olympic Games of the Modern Age, which are a global mega-event, which is "owned" by the IOC, and governed by the Olympic Charter, a document accepted by the entire Olympic Movement, which comprises dozens of sports federations, and the over 200 National Olympic Committees recognised by the IOC. It is likewise obvious that many more people are involved in the Olympic Games than were involved in the original Games. For example, there were no sport entrepreneurs, or marketing professionals, in antiquity. It is also evident that there was no pyramidal associative sport structure, with the IOC at its apex and the international federations, continental confederations, national federations, district/regional associations, clubs and individual sportspersons ranked hierarchically under it. The legal acquis of antiquity also cannot be compared with the multiplicity of norms that now exist at the various levels, bylaws, regulations, codes and other texts regarding a wide range of different matters, such as disciplinary and ethical issues, transfers, television broadcast rights, electoral issues, financial, technological and intellectual property obligations, and many other requirements that exist because of the multiple close interconnections that now exist between sport and business. However, we nevertheless consider that the roots and source of the contemporary structure are to be found and were created at Olympia with the birth of the Olympic Games.

As far as we are aware, the thesis propounded in this chapter has no precedent in legal theory. There are, however, a few exceptions that see the "roots" of contemporary sport law in Roman Law, that is, in the Justinian Code, for example, recent positions, such as those of Goce NAUMOVSKI,[20] and more particularly, less recent positions such as those of the brilliant Italian legal theorist, Ugo GUALAZZINI.[21] GUALAZZINI referred to a sporting event as a legal transaction, that exists within the context of a general legal order, with a *praxis* that imposes a fairly standard discipline, with an ethical profile, in which the rules that characterised the entire Games were accepted, and were combined with other rules of a penal nature. According to those authors, the Games, as a sporting event, were a legal transaction in a context of a general legal order, with a praxis that imposed a fairly standard discipline, with an ethical profile. The Games rules were generally transferred by tradition, and governed the game as it was played, via the imposition of penalties and the establishment the scoring criteria, were accepted, and were combined with other rules of a penal nature. Other authors refer to a birth of "*Roman sport law*",[22] which is viewed as "*an ordered, and coherent system that governed a very important aspect of the economic, political, and popular life of the empire*", on the assumption that law and sport are "*two sides of the same vital reality, and walk hand-in-hand*".

However, it is our view that it all started in Ancient Greece. We know that, for the Romans, sport was a spectacle, it was entertainment, and was professionalised, and included extreme examples such as gladiatorial combats. It is therefore unsurprising that during the Roman period, and unlike the Greek case, there was a true division between public and private law as applied to sport, or that phenomena such as sports betting, civil liability applied to sport, and recourse to loan contracts, as a way of sponsoring athletes, existed. The development, systemisation and codification of law, in general, and sport law, in particular, was, in fact, more advanced in Rome, than in Greece. But this does not gainsay the fact that a sport law had arisen, previously, in Greece, although no legal theorist appears to have adopted this position.

We consider that this lacuna in legal theory, which this chapter modestly seeks to resolve, or mitigate, is fundamentally a result of the polysemic nature of sport, as outlined earlier. Moreover, in the sport sciences, in general, and in the history of sport, in particular, there is a difference of opinion about when sport first emerged. Moreover, we are well aware even among those historians, who consider that sport first emerged in Ancient Egypt, in 4000 BCE, or China, in 3000 BCE, there is no consensus that this sport (which already existed autonomously from games), and was essentially associated with religious ceremonies, was, or was not, intrinsically characterised by rules. It is therefore difficult, or risky, to assert that sport law existed.

Moreover, the truth is that this issue has never merited the real interest or attention of legal theorists of sport, because their primary, if not sole, concern, for a long time, was merely to study it, and/or ensure the existence of sport law as an autonomous branch of the law. As this autonomisation has only occurred in recent decades, the trend has always been to consider that sport law is something that has emerged in the 20th century, or, at most, that emerged in its primitive state in the late 19th century, with the birth of the first international sports federations, and the adoption of the corresponding bylaws and regulations.

The thesis to be proved

The thesis that we intend to prove, that is, the aim of this chapter, is that given the fact, already demonstrated, that there can be no competition without rules, sport law first emerged at Olympia, at the Olympic Games of Antiquity, that is, at the first major sports competition in the History of Humanity. For, as stated by Fernando FERREIRA,[23] "*it was in Ancient Greece that physical exercises and athletic games first become an institution, and something that was part of the national customs and life, and acquired educational, religious, and aesthetic characteristics.* This marked a probable transition from sport practices [according to the author, in Egypt; China; India; Persia; Japan; and Tibet], *merely probable, because there are no descriptions of these older activities prior to the Greeks, to the first properly organised competitions, that took place at predetermined times, according to defined rules, and under the control of judges.*" We stress these three factors: rules, organisation and judges.

The importance of competition in Ancient Greece, particularly at Olympia, and its special connection with law, was a Greek idiosyncrasy, as is shown by the famous episode of King Endimion's appointment of his successor, which is recounted by José Manuel MEIRIM,[24] based on Bernard JEU: "*There are some who claim, based on the primitive imagination, that the sports procedure arose as an archaic form of political law. The proximity of law and sport, at their source, explains, for example, why a king would be appointed via recourse to a race. A race can decide royalty. ENDYMION caused his four sons to dispute the succession to the throne and it was thus that competitive sporting prowess is a source of truth.*"

Sport law at Olympus

The law in Ancient Greece: brief account of the Olympic Games of Antiquity and their effects

The first Olympic Games of Antiquity were held in 796 BCE at Olympia, in Hellas (which was the name of Greece, at the time).

Greece was divided into city-states, each of which was an independent state, with its own laws, even though there was a single Hellenic community in religious, political, social and cultural terms.

Unlike the Romans, the Greeks did not create a science of law, or initiate a systematic elaboration of legal concepts, or codify the law. The Greeks were not concerned to create a unitary law-governed system. However, this does not mean that the Greeks regarded law as of secondary importance. They acknowledged its educational function, as both Plato and Aristotle noted, in their time. Plato and Aristotle were not just great philosophers. They were also great athletes, who argued that obedience to law was precisely one of the means whereby the citizenry could be educated. Accordingly, the legislative process was an eminently noble activity, and an obligation of the wise, in which legislators were educators.

For the Greeks, the law was also a form of harmonious coexistence of the citizenry. Accordingly, it was therefore evident that they wished to organise human life through law, legality and the reduction of norms publicised in written form, so as to be accessible to all, and to provide all citizens with the necessary legal clarity and certainty. The great legislators, such as Draco, Solon, Lycurgus or Clisthenes, played a fundamental role in this process, and some of them were directly involved in Olympic matters, as we will see.

But Greek law is not just explained in terms of human will. There is an additional aspect, which is based on the close proximity of law and religion, which had an obvious impact on the normative structuring of the Olympic Games, indeed the Games were called Olympic, because the Olympians were the Gods of Olympus.

Religion was an integral part of all social life in Ancient Greece. The law and sport were closely bound to a sort of "*civic religion*", to adopt the words of Elena PÉREZ MARTIN.[25] This necessarily impacted the Olympic Games and its inherent norms. The stadium, the hippodrome and all other sports infrastructures were sacred; and all sport events and ceremonies had religious connotations. The fundamental reason for participation in the Games was to please the gods, who were superhuman beings, particularly Zeus, the God of the Gods, in order not to annoy them, or provoke their vengeance. The choice of Olympia, the spiritual centre of the Hellenic world, as the locus of the Games, therefore made complete sense.

Emanuele STOLFI[26] writes that "*Zeus was clothed in the nomos*", that is, the God of the Gods clothed himself in the law, and commanded all earthly life in such a way that, to use the words of STOLFI, the legal culture of Ancient Greece was constructed "*from Olympus to the polis*". The law was given by God to Man, higher moral rules reached the city via a Natural Law, from which men created the Law of the City. Earthly law therefore came from an external source and was based on divine commands.

Thus was the Justice of Zeus imposed. This justice was not based on a code of laws but was nevertheless no mystery to the legislators. In practice, authority was based on the sacred nature of the laws. The citizens in an Assembly, or any other legislative body, merely ratified these laws, in civil terms. Laws were divine at source and applied directly to Man, that is, Greek divine will was materialised and expressed through human will. When Man wrote the law, it already had a source, which was Olympus. The human task was therefore nothing more than the manifestation of a transcendent will, the conversion of a Natural Law, and communication to the earthly world of something that was metaphysical, religious and even cosmic. Religious laws were the first laws and determined all others. Paulo FERREIRA DA CUNHA,[27] quoting Sebastião CRUZ, provides a happy synthesis: "*Greek justice would look to the heavens (or Olympus) for inspiration, but with its eyes wide open.*"

It was therefore in this context that the Olympic Games arose in Ancient Greece, in what Bernardo MANZANO[28] describes as a symbiosis between Human Law and Divine Law, which needed precise rules and competent judges, that is, priests. According to this author, the Olympic Games were sustained by the Gods of Olympus, and this was not unrelated to the fact that one of the purposes of the Games of Antiquity was to seek peace, as is also true of the modern Games, which, according to the Olympic Charter, are intended to promote a peaceful society and a peaceful world.

Law in the preparation of the Olympic Games of Antiquity

The Greeks had recourse to law, firstly in order to create conditions "under the auspices of public authority"[29] in which the Games could be held, via the signing of a Treaty between the states of Elis, Sparta and Pisa, referred to as the Sacred Truce, and also to create the conditions necessary for the training and selection of the athletes, on equal terms, by fixing a ten-month training period immediately preceding the opening of the Games, and a 30-day period prior to the beginning of the Games during which all athletes were required to register.

The Sacred Truce (Olympic Truce)

In 884 BCE, Iphitus, King of Elis, after consulting the Delphic oracle, and being advised by Pythia to make peace with the neighbouring peoples, concluded a historic Pan-Hellenic treaty, at Olympia, which was neutral territory, with Cleisthenes, King of Pisa, and Lycurgus, King of Sparta, also a famous legislator, which instituted the *Ekecheiria,* or Sacred Truce.

As can be seen from the date, this Treaty was signed 108 years before the first Olympic Games. Accordingly, it only makes sense to call it the Olympic Truce once it had a practical application in relation to the Olympic Games. Accordingly, each Olympiad, that is, the period that precedes each Olympic Games, commenced with a public proclamation, in all Greek cities, by the spondophoroi, the sacred heralds, the "messengers of peace" chosen from among the Greek aristocracy. However, there is no consensus in the sources regarding the length of the Truce. Opinions vary between one, three and even ten months before the beginning of the Games (with the length of the Truce increasing as the Games became more important, and more competitors and spectators began to arrive from increasingly distant places). There are also conflicting opinions regarding the end of the Truce, which, for some, ended at the same time as the Games, and for others, continued after that date.

According to Pausanias, the text of the Treaty, which was signed in circular lines on a copper disc, and was kept at a sacred location, that is, the Temple of the Goddess Hera (Zeus' official wife), until at least the 2nd century BCE, was as follows: "*Olympia is a sacred place. Whoever dares to tread this soil with his army shall be vituperated as a heretic. Whoever fails to avenge a crime when it is in his power to do so, is as iniquitous.*"

According to some, this Treaty was a peace treaty, others maintain that it was merely an armistice, that is, an agreement to refrain from recourse to arms during a certain period, that is, a temporary cessation of hostilities, a truce, or a publicly agreed, acknowledged and observed inviolability of persons, territories and objects, without belligerence. Paradoxically, peace broke out during the period prior to a sport event, although sport itself was a powerful instrument of military preparation.

In practice, the Truce was a formal proclamation of the inviolability of the regions in which religious festivals and sports competitions were taking place. The Truce was specifically applied to the Olympic Games, via a declaration that the territory of Elis was neutral, inviolable and sacred. The Truce required troops that entered Elis to surrender their arms, which they could only recover on leaving Elis, as in capitulation agreements, which include an appeal to the good faith of the adversaries. This gave freedom of movement and immunity to all those who travelled to Olympia, that is, athletes, coaches, delegations, spectators, merchants and pilgrims, in general, even when passing through the territories of hostile cities, or of cities that were at war with the travellers' cities.

The Olympic Truce proved to be an effective legal instrument that made it possible for the Games to take place, by seeking a divine peace, like what has happened at the Olympic Games of the Modern Age, which have only been cancelled twice, once for each of the two world wars. Nevertheless, as we shall see, there were still a few cases of violation of the Olympic Truce, which were duly punished.

We can already conclude that the referred Treaty was a legal tool to ensure peace as a precondition for holding the Olympic Games.

The obligatory ten-month period prior to the event

The rules adopted to ensure initial theoretical equality of opportunity between all competing athletes are a second example of recourse to law to facilitate the start of the Olympic Games (which is now much referred to as the *par conditio* principle) and necessarily involves respect for these rules, which imposes strict compliance with an obligatory ten-month pre-event training period, on all athletes. For the same reason, all athletes were required to report in Elis, a city located 57 km from Olympia, one month prior to the start of the Games, in order to undergo a joint and simultaneous training control, in uniform infrastructural conditions, which included access to identical human resources, and a dietary regime. Only in this way could equality, equal conditions and effective comparison, or measurement, of forces between adversaries, be ensured.

The Aquis of the Olympic Games of Antiquity

The existence of different duly ranked sources of law

The creation of the rules governing the Olympic Games of Antiquity, which Pindarus describes as the "Laws of Zeus" (*themites Dios*), was attributed to Heracles, most of which were "*discovered by archaeologists*",[30] although there is, as yet no solid proof of this. It seems to be clear that the rules evolved over successive Olympiads. Most sources indicate that this legislative role was attributed to the *nomographoi*, who were a special committee of legislators, or a group of jurists, who worked under the auspices of the Government of Elis. Herodotus writes that these rules, which already amounted to a "*very complex Olympic legislation*",[31] had been ordered from the Egyptian sages, during the reign of Psammis. Álvaro MELO FILHO[32] writes that the rules in question "*were submitted to the sages and philosophers for consideration, which indicates the rules' public importance and social transcendence*". We stress that this late-lamented and unequalled Brazilian jurist is perhaps the only author we know of, worldwide, who refers to the existence of a sport law in the Olympic Games of Antiquity, although he does so while referring to the existence of "*rules of a rudimentary sport law*" in Ancient Greece.

But what were these rules? These rules were the "canons" or "Fundamental Laws of Olympia" (*olympiakos nomos*), which comprised three hierarchically ranked categories, that is, the "Olympic Laws"; the "Olympic Regulations" and the "Event Rules".

The "Olympic Laws", which ranked highest and provided the logical and formal framework for the lower level rules, were engraved on bronze plates, which were kept at the permanent headquarters of the Olympic Council, or Senate, that is, the *Bouleuterion.*

Ranked immediately below the Olympic Laws were the "Olympic Regulations" which implemented, or developed, the "Olympic Laws", in more programmatic rules regarding the specific features of the various sports, which were gradually included in the Games Programme.

These rules were equivalent to the current "Test Event Regulations" or "Competition Regulations" which are approved for the organisation of all competitions, such as Local Tournaments, National Championships, European Championships, World Cups, or even the Olympic Games of the Modern Age. These are the rules to which competitors submit when they compete in an event, which are drawn up and applied by the competition organiser, and which, in the most extreme cases, can result in disqualification, or expulsion from the competition. These rules apply while a sports game is ongoing. These rules fixed matters such as the duration of the Games, which was initially one day, but was later finally fixed as five days, and the Games Programme, that is, the various sports included in the Games, which increased in number over time, to 23. For example, the stadion (the only event included in all of the first 13 Games), the diaulos (a double-stadion race), the dolichos (a 24-stadion race), wrestling, pentathlon (discus, long jump, javelin, stadion and wrestling), boxing, quadriga chariot racing, horse races and the pankration.

Finally, the "Event Rules", which, in the Olympic Games of Antiquity, were the more specific, or particular, rules. For example, these rules concerned issues regarding the conduct of events, particularly the technical rules of the various sports, that is, the "rules of the game", rules linked to sports acts, and the conduct of the event, that is, rules limited to a specific event. These were foundational rules that define each sport (such as those which are currently the province of the various sport federations), rules regarding sport-related conduct (the obligations of the athletes, which together define the corresponding sport) which, at that time, included rules regarding the distances to be run, the techniques to be used, the criteria applicable in the determination of the winner, the existence, or non-existence, of preliminary heats, prohibited blows, permitted interruptions, false starts and other issues. It is interesting to note that only first place was decided, as there were no runners-up, and there was no other classification factor, awarding of points or determination of records. The rules included technical specifications such as the dimensions of the sports ground (e.g. the size of the stadium or the hippodrome), and the nature and physical composition of the equipment used, such as shape, weight or size, although the records indicate some uniformity issues in this area. Curiously, there was also great concern regarding what athletes could not do during the Games. This involved the prohibition of the following conduct: (i) intentional or negligent killing of the opponent,[33] that is, in wrestling or boxing contests; (ii) pushing the opponent, or recourse to unfair conduct; (iii) corruption and intimidation of opponents and umpires/judges; and (iv) public protests against decisions of umpires/judges.

The relevance of the eligibility rules

The most comprehensive and detailed rules in the Olympic Games of Antiquity were the eligibility rules, that is, the rules that established the requirements regarding admission to, or participation in, events, and detailed the procedure for the selection of athletes, which, adopting the terms now used, gave permission to compete in the event, a power, which is now exercised by the international sports federations, regarding selection for the modern Olympic Games.

It is noted that the eligibility rules are still important today. For instance, the UEFA Financial Fair Play Regulation, which introduces a range of differing criteria, regarding sport, infrastructures, human resources, management, legal, and financial matters, which must be complied with in order to compete in competitions organised by UEFA; rules that prohibit, or limit, participation by foreigners; rules that limit participation according to physical characteristics, such as weight (especially in combat sports), intersex athletes/hyperandrogenism issues;[34] or the recent and controversial rules regarding the admission of paralympic athletes, who use prostheses,[35] and transgender athletes,[36] as competitors in the Olympic Games.

Research reveals that participation in the Olympic Games of Antiquity was subject to a wide and varied range of "conditions", which José Pedro Martins[37] classifies as "*very restrictive*", even citing José Esteves, to the effect that they are, in some cases, "*discriminatory*",[38] something that clearly differs from the modern rules, in the Olympic Charter, which not only enshrines sport as a human right but advocates the principle of non-discrimination.

For example, *only free citizens could take part in the Games*, whatever their social status, although given the costs of training and travel, participation was far more accessible to the citizens from the highest classes, who had more time, and, above all, more money.

Furthermore, *only Greeks could take part in the Games*. The athletes had to be the legitimate sons of Greek citizens, racially pure, without any mixed-race heritage, that is, of Greek maternal and paternal lineage, as confirmed by the birth records of the city of origin. This was somewhat difficult to prove given the rudimentary nature of the public archives at that time, which raises the possibility that false genealogies may have been submitted. Foreigners were viewed as hostile and could therefore never take part in the Games. There were three types of foreigners: the isoteloi, metics and barbarians. Barbarians were completely unrelated to the Hellenic community (who had no rights, and could be enslaved) and were viewed as hostile and could therefore never compete in the Games. In fact, in Classical Antiquity, foreigners originally had no legal personality, and therefore no rights or obligations. Their legal status was the same as that of a thing, and their owner had the rights of life, or death, regarding them. However, treaties were gradually made with foreign cities, but only in limited terms. Given the fact that the slave class, which was very oppressed and numerous in Greece, had arisen because of a lack of a sufficient workforce, and via the exercise of rights of war, it is easily understood how this rule limited the available pool of potential athletes, who could compete in the Games. Only after the conquest of Greece by the Romans (Olympia became a Roman province in 146 CE, after the destruction of Corinth by the Roman army), did the first non-Greeks participate in the Olympic Games,[39] which thus lost their Pan-Hellenic character and spirit, although the Games continued to be held. There was apparently only one occasion when the Games were not held at Olympia, but in Rome in 80 BCE, on the occasion of the 175th Olympiad.

Likewise, *only men could compete in the Games, from which women were excluded.*[40] This can be explained by the prevailing cultural view of the role of women, or by the idea that the Games had a major connection with military training, from which women were also excluded. The penalty for the violation of this ban was death, and the woman concerned was thrown from the Typaion rock. One violation of this rule was detected: Kallipateira, the daughter of Diagoras of Rhodes, entered the stadium concealed under a tunic, in the guise of a male trainer. She did this in order to watch her son, Peisidoros, who took part in, and won, a boxing match, which she did seated on the benches as her son's supposed trainer. When her son won, Kallipateira was unable to contain her joy and jumped into the arena to embrace her son, at which the tunic fell, thus revealing her identity. The Olympic Senate, which, as we shall see, played a central role, particularly in the "sport justice" of the time, was convened urgently, and absolved and pardoned Kallipateira on the grounds that she was the daughter, sister and mother of Olympic champions. The sole exception to the ban on the participation of women was in horse races. This had a logical explanation, as the winner was not the chariot driver, but the owner of the horses. This explains how Princess Cyniske of Sparta came to be an Olympic champion at the 96th and 97th Olympiad, in 396 BCE and 392 BCE. Likewise, the presence of women at the Games was prohibited.[41] The only exception to this rule was the priestess of Demeter Carmine, the Harvest Goddess, who wore a white tunic and sat facing the judges, on the opposite side of the stadium.

Similarly, citizens, whose rights of citizenship had been forfeited because of the commission of a civil or religious offence, could not take part in the Games. Athletes, who had ever been convicted could not compete in the Games, for example, those guilty of murder or negligent homicide. Basically, athletes on whom the penalty of athymia, that is, withdrawal of civil rights, has been imposed, because of a serious offence, were banned from the Games, as were athletes guilty of sacrilege.

Athletes guilty of blasphemy were likewise banned from the Games.

As already demonstrated, participation in the Games was also dependent on compliance with an obligatory registration time limit, which required athletes to register in a special list, the *leucoma*, one month prior to the Games.

Athletes who arrived late for the Games were also excluded, unless they provided an acceptable explanation for their late arrival. For example, in 93 CE, Apollonius, a boxer from Alexandria, attributed his late arrival to the delayed arrival of his ship, because of adverse winds in the Cyclades. This explanation was not accepted because Apollonios' adversary and co-citizen, Heraclides, stated that Apollonius had arrived late because he had gone to collect a prize won at another sports event. It appears from this incident that denunciations occurred and were permitted. Other reasons for late arrival at the Games that were frequently invoked were illness, piracy, robbery and shipwreck, all of which had to be duly proved.

Likewise, athletes who had not paid taxes demanded by the state were also excluded from the Games. This rule was also an indirect means to coerce tax debtors to pay their taxes.

In events subject to age requirements regarding[42] citizens, or horses, *it was necessary to prove inclusion in the respective category* – youth or adult; horse or colt, although this proof was difficult because there were no birth records at that time. This meant that appearance was inevitably the decisive criterion.

Athletes were also required to compete naked. Some explain this requirement as a matter of decency. Others claim that nakedness was intended as a contrast with barbarians for whom nakedness was a mark of shame. There are records that refer to the case of Kallipateira as the real reason athletes and trainers had to be naked, but that explanation is far from consensual. There are also those who view the nakedness rule as a guarantee of equality, which, according to tradition, arose following the case of Orsippus, who, in 724 BCE, removed his loincloth in order to be faster and more agile. At that time, there was a view that sports equipment could affect athletic performance. It was therefore concluded that equality between competitors could be ensured, either by all athletes using the same equipment or by a ban on equipment, with the latter option being adopted. This is the origin of the current concern, on which international sports federations approval of equipment, and the prohibition of the use of clothing, footwear or other sports material that could give a competitive advantage, is based.

It is finally noteworthy that while most sources point to the fact that competition in the Games was free of charge, that is, there was no registration fee, some sources refer to a *requirement that athletes must hail from a city pacified by Zeus* that paid a certain tribute.

The preservation of Sports Ethics

THE FIGHT AGAINST CORRUPTION

As referred to below, the opening of the Games was preceded by the proclamation of an oath, violation of which was perjury. The fact that the oath refers to a commitment that the various sports actors would not become involved in acts of corruption, indicates that corrupt practices that sought to distort the results of events did exist, and that the oath was intended to prevent and combat this scourge.

What was the reason for such conduct at that time? Philostratus saw the reason for this phenomenon as a weakening of customs, and a pleasure-seeking attitude that arose among athletes, because of their corrupt lust for money, and the consequent practice of buying and selling victories.[43] The situation was also vitiated by the conduct of coaches and representatives, who had little concern for their own ethics, or the ethics of athletes, and whose major concern was their own gain. There is also another possible explanation, that is, some athletes, who were accustomed to a luxurious life, preferred to lose the Games voluntarily, in exchange for a good bribe. There is yet another possible explanation, that is, that corruption did not result in the forfeiture of the winner's title and crown, even though it involved a heavy penalty. Furthermore, we cannot overlook another aspect that could explain the corruption, that is, the rivalry between cities, and political disputes, as the crowning ceremonies involved the exaltation of the athlete, his father, and the city/community to which they belonged. The simpler explanation, given by the Greek philosopher Lucianus, also cannot be excluded, that is, that corruption could simply be a consequence of the athlete's dishonesty, the desire to win at any price, or of despair that causes athletes to cheat.[44] José ESTEVES[45] provides the following overall view: "*And while it is true that the Olympic Games regulations provided that only athletes free of moral stain could be admitted to the Games, we also know, from contemporary accounts, how bribery and similar conduct impinged on the competition for the valued prizes. This naturally has to be viewed against a social background in which other members of the human race were not regarded as brothers, or colleagues, but were viewed as alien and 'an enemy' to be eliminated.*"

Various cases of corruption occurred at the Olympic Games of Antiquity. The following are some of the main cases. There was a scandal in 396 BCE regarding a race. Two judges decided in favour of an Eleusinian athlete, and the third judge decided in favour of an Ambracian athlete. The athlete from Ambracia did not accept the judges' decision and appealed to the Olympic Senate, which decided in his favour. However, as it was not possible to reverse the result of the race, the award of the victory to his opponent, who had even celebrated it by erecting a statue, still stood. Nevertheless, the two judges were sanctioned. In 388 BCE, a boxer paid three other competitors, one of whom was the reigning champion, to allow him to win the trophy. The judges punished the four athletes and the proceeds of the fines, which amounted to about ten times the annual salary of an artisan, were applied to fund the erection of six bronze statues dedicated to Zeus, in Altis, on which the names of the offenders and the nature of their offence were inscribed. One of the boxers was expelled from his city. In 332 BCE, a pentathlon athlete attempted to pay his opponents not to put up much of a fight in the event, and the offence was detected. The city of Athens sent its best orator and politician, Hypereides, to Elis to try to forestall the imposition of a penalty on the athlete, but without success. As the athlete was insolvent, and the athlete's city, Athens in this case, was jointly liable to pay the fine imposed, it refused to pay and made a public announcement that it would boycott the next Olympic Games. However, the city of Athens did pay in the end, apparently after the Delphic oracle had been consulted. This is a good example of how rules and judgements were seen as of divine origin, and something fearsome, that inculcated terror. This explains the statement that *"the maximum representative of legalism is Apollo* [the representative of Zeus], *whose decisions were made known via the Delphic oracle."*[46] There are reports of pre-agreed victories, in 125 BCE, which led to the punishment of two Alexandrian boxers. In 102 BCE, there was another scandal, which concerned a horse race won by an owner, who was also a judge. Following this case, judges were prohibited from competing in horse races. In 68 BCE, two athletes from Rhodes were punished for fixing the result of an event in exchange for money. In 12 BCE, there was a case of attempted corruption, which involved the fathers of two boxers. The father of one of the boxers bribed the father of the other to ensure that his son would let the son of the first father win. The fathers were convicted and ordered to erect a statue of Zeus, on the left and right of the entrance to the Olympic Stadium. These statues erected as an anti-corruption penalty were known as *zanes*,[47] and they bore the names of the guilty and the facts of the conviction. This was not only an attempt to deter other competitors but also intended to instil fear (as a lesson to all Greeks, and not just the guilty parties). During the Roman period, Emperor Nero bribed the umpires/judges to proclaim him the winner, despite the fact that he had fallen in the hippodrome when driving a ten-horse chariot. However, he was subsequently required to repay the sum of 250,000 drachmas improperly received.

DOPING AS AN UNTYPIFIED OFFENCE

Although there was previously a legal definition of doping, such a definition no longer exists, as the option adopted in the WADA World Anti-Doping Code was to list violations of the anti-doping rules. These violations include the use of prohibited substances, which improve athlete performance pharmacologically, artificially and/or non-endogenously, and the use of prohibited methods.

Obviously, the athletes of Classical Antiquity did not use drugs to artificially improve their sporting performance, but this does not mean that they did not use certain products to improve their results. For example, just as athletes these days have recourse to autotransfusion, athletes in Ancient Greece used similar methods to manipulate their bodies. For example,

Athletes consumed mushrooms and plant and seed extracts to improve their performance, and drank mead to enhance their central nervous systems. Likewise, and as in primitive cultures, blood had a central role, athletes ate a lot of meat, which varied according to their sport. For example, jumpers ate goat meat; discus and javelin throwers, and boxers preferred bull testicles; while wrestlers, particularly those who fought in the heavier weight categories, preferred fatty pork. There are also records that in the 5th century BCE, in the days of Hippocrates, long-distance runners ingested various plants that they cooked and burnt, and used astringent and haemostatic acids, before the race, to prevent congestion of the spleen, a painful condition that causes the spleen to harden. Herbs, such as horsetail, and plants with stimulant properties, such as ephedra, were also used.

Everything referred to earlier would clearly fall within the area of diet and nutrition and not involve the use of prohibited substances, or any breach of the law, or any ethical considerations. The only record of such a matter being the subject of a legal prohibition is a ban on the pre-competition consumption of alcoholic beverages by athletes, which was apparently instituted in the 7th century BCE, by Lycurgus, King of Sparta, although the sources regarding this do not agree. This ban put an end to a habit that while allowing athletes to relax before their events, also posed a risk to their physical integrity. Some consider this ban to be the *"first anti-doping control in history"*.[48] Although this measure was a ban rather than a control, the legal assets it protected, that is, sports ethics and public health, were clearly the same as those protected by the contemporary fight against doping.

As far as methods now classified as prohibited are concerned, some athletes removed their spleens, when they became inflamed and caused severe pain, in order not to harm their performance and to ensure agility and speed. There were also cases of mutilation of the penis (an alternative to sexual continence and cold baths, which were also used to increase performance).

However, the real concern of the umpires/judges was equality between all contestants. This was ensured by the ten-month period referred to earlier, during which all athletes had the same training conditions, and their nutrition was monitored, in order to prevent the use of secret recipes, or potions, to promote muscle growth, and the use of products that were deemed improper, or which only some athletes were in a position to use, and were therefore considered to amount to an unfair advantage.

ENDOGENOUS AND EXOGENOUS VIOLENCE

As far as violence in sport is concerned, that is, endogenous violence, between athletes during the competition, it is noted that this was generally tolerated in the Olympic Games of Antiquity, that is, "*the competition regulations of that time were very benign.*"[49] The rules permitted recourse to methods that amounted to, or resulted in, fractures, or blows, to sensitive parts of the body. The pankration was the major example of this consensual violence. For, although biting of the genitals, severing of fingers, and gouging of eyes were prohibited, there were many deaths, and broken fingers, and devastating blows to the head from above were frequent. There were few restrictions in terms of the method of the combats. As to the duration, combats could last many hours, until the fighters were rendered unconscious, yielded or died.

As regards exogenous violence, that is, spectator violence linked to, or associated with, sport, there are testimonies of the not infrequent occurrence of fights, particularly in the stadium, which had no seating and could accommodate a maximum of 50,000 spectators. This situation has contemporary parallels, such as the reports of spectators, who throw dangerous objects onto the field of play, to target players, who break the rules, notwithstanding the fact that this is the role of referees/judges and the police.

The Olympic Games of Antiquity were policed by the *alytes* (guardians of the sanctuary) or *mastigophoroi*, who acted under the auspices of the Alitarch, a senior magistrate, whose role was that of Chief, Officer or Commissioner of Police, that is, his role was to ensure public order. This police force could use rods, and whips, to control offenders. The alytes also had a more preventive role, similar to that of contemporary *stewards*, that is, they placed spectators in the stadium and ensured that they did not go beyond the barriers that separated spectators from the part of the stadium where the events took place. João LYRA FILHO[50] argues as follows, regarding the said policing: "The *Hellenic tradition contains the first sign of a role of public authority in the development of sport law. For, as we have already stated, sport feeds a good part of the expressions of social life, and therefore, like all activity of social life, requires a legal structure that governs its institutional organisation.*"

THE RULES REGARDING CONFLICTS OF INTEREST

In equestrian events, umpires/judges, who could initially also be owners of horses, were both trainers and competitors. However, in 364 BCE, following the victory of two umpires/judges in two equestrian events, it was decided that no umpire/judge would be permitted to compete as an owner.

Accordingly, we can see that, in Ancient Greece, there were already rules of conduct, deontological concerns and the institution of disqualification criteria to avoid conflicts of interest. Such concerns are currently included in the Ethic Codes and Codes of Conduct of various sports organisations. This is yet another example of the essential role of Law in the organisation of sport, both on and off the field of play.

The multiplicity of persons involved in the Olympic Games of Antiquity and their acceptance of the binding nature of the applicable rules

Persons

The Olympic Games of Antiquity involved a multiplicity of persons, who would today be referred to as sports actors, particularly athletes (who all registered for the Games in their own names, as there were no teams), trainers (whose role also included tasks now performed by physicians and nutritionists) and umpires/judges.

The issue of the amateur or professional status of **athletes** did not arise. The Greeks made no distinction between amateur and professional athletes. The word *athlea* meant someone, who competes for a prize.

Officially, the prize (*athlos*) was not material but was rather a crown of wild olive foliage (*kotinos*), which symbolised virtue, courage and glory, and seemed to indicate a preference for amateurism. However, as Constantino FERNANDES,[51] the first major Portuguese scholar of sport law, notes, *"[i]n Ancient Greece, the athletes that competed in the Olympic Games, especially after the 4th century BCE, had many privileges . . ., and according to some historians, were sometimes professional athletes . . .. However, it is almost considered an outrage to suggest that professionalism existed in classical Olympism.*" Nevertheless, the author is correct, there were, in fact, prizes that were not mere honorific awards, but which amounted to money's worth, many of them typical of professionalism, for example, (i) Gold or silver objects; (ii) the privilege of fighting alongside the king; (iii) land; (iv) exemption from military service; (v) an official reception on the return home; (vi) houses; (vii) tax exemptions; (viii) permanent pensions; (ix) a place of prominence at all public events and ceremonies; (x) statues in local squares and monuments, venerated as symbols of heroism[52]; (xi) a special anthem; (xii) mausoleums; (xiii) free meals for the rest of the athlete's life; (xiv) appointment as a member of the governing bodies of the polis; (xv) immunity from imprisonment; (xvi) immortality of the winner, as ensured by odes to his victory, written by poets; (xvii) coining of coins by rulers and kings to immortalise victories, particular in equestrian events; (xviii) heroification via a *post-mortem* cult; and (xix) coins.

A decision was made in 592 BCE, at the 47th Olympiad, by Solon, a statesman, legislator and poet, regarding prize money, which involved the fixing of a maximum limit of 500 drachmas regarding the prizes to be awarded by the Athenian Government to the winners of the Olympic Games. This was a considerable amount, as an artisan, who was at the top of the socio-professional pyramid, had the daily income of one drachma. Despite the fact that the said amount was a maximum limit, it was nevertheless an obvious reward, a stimulus to sport, and legislative recognition that reflected recognition of the educational value of the art of the body.[53] In any event, this limitation was also understood as a form of containment of public expenditure, during a public spending crisis,[54] and was also perceived as a legal way to standardise prizes, and limit the size of the aristocracy, and a way to use public funds for another purpose, that is, to support the widows and children of patriots killed in wars.

Trainers can be divided into three categories: *paidotribes*, who were experienced veteran athletes, who had theoretical training, whose role was similar to that of contemporary physical education teachers; *gymnastes* – trainers of professional athletes, who applied techniques and *aleiptes* – who anointed athletes with oil for muscle massage.

Philostratus wrote in the 2nd century CE, about a Gymnastics Treaty, which states that trainers exploited athletes financially, by charging them exaggerated amounts,[55] which shows that some of these trainers were professionals.

There are also accounts of what would now be referred to as a trainer transfer, regarding a trainer called Demokenes, who moved from Kroton to Aegina to earn 12 times more than an average Greek worker.

Umpires and judges, that is, the *hellanoidikai*, which literally means "judges of the Greeks", a title that was given at Olympia to *agonothetes*, the magistrates, who were the "*depositaries of the Olympic laws*",[56] and had the power to correct, or sanction, the various actors involved in the Games, in order to ensure that the Games proceeded in accordance with the rules. The hellanoidikai were therefore equivalent to the current umpires, although their duties were much more extensive.

Before they performed the said duties at the Games, the hellanoidikai monitored the athletes during the obligatory preliminary ten-month period. The hellanoidikai validated the registration of all eligible athletes one month before the Games. They inspected all infrastructures, animals and athletes, and even cleaned the location, repaired statues and spread sand, in the latter case, with the assistance of the athletes. They also supervised the training of the athletes, which took place in the gymnasium, that is, in the palaestra. They received sacraments and performed purifications. The hellanoidikai also performed a wide range of management, organisational, and even protocolary tasks, which would these days fall to an Organising Committee. They were also responsible for ensuring public order. The hellanoidikai also had the power to add events to, or delete events from, the Games Programme, and the power to alter the order of events.[57] The hellanoidikai were of course also judges and handed down disciplinary decisions regarding compliance with the various Olympic Laws. The hellanoidikai were also responsible for ensuring strict performance of rites and strict compliance with the rules, until the end of the event. It is noteworthy, particularly because this was "*a period in the rules were first being developed*",[58] that the hellanoidikai also evaluated the character and morality of the athletes, to ensure that their dignity matched the great reputation of the Olympic sanctuary. Finally, the hellanoidikai had the power to engrave the winners' names on an official catalogue that was permanently displayed in the gymnasium. It can therefore be stated that the role of the hellanoidikai was managerial, technical, judicial and even one of priesthood. Delphine CONNES refers to this as a "*public sport law*"[59] which was enforced by priests and magistrates.

It is difficult to find a consensus in the sources about various issues regarding these supreme judges of the Games. Firstly, and regarding the date when the hellanoidikai first appeared, there are those who state that their role was initially performed by Eleusinian priests, and that magistrates only began to perform those duties in 400 BCE. However, there are other indications that the hellanoidikai date back to the beginning of the Games. There is likewise no consensus regarding the number of hellanoidikai. There are records of a minimum number of one, or two, and of a maximum of ten, or 12. However, it seems certain that the number varied from time to time, with most sources indicating that the number was fixed at ten, at some point, there is also no unanimity on whether membership of the hellanoidikai was hereditary, awarded by the drawing of lots, or the result of selection, or election. While there are some references to election, other sources state that the term of office of the hellanoidikai coincided with each Olympiad (four years), yet others indicate that their term of office was lifelong.

The hellanoidikai were high-status, and therefore munificent, members of the Eleusinian nobility. They even bore some part of the costs of the Games, which meant that spectators did not have to purchase an entrance ticket. They wore purple tunics. Purple was a symbol of greatness, dignity, authority and royalty. They also wore laurel crowns. The hellanoidikai worked under the aegis of the *nomophylakes*, the "Guardians of the Laws", who instructed them regarding the applicable rules, and were aided by the *bouleutes*, the members of the Olympic Senate, or Council, and by auxiliary umpires during events. The hellanoidikai were also aided by the *rabdoukoi* ("rod bearers"), who used their rods to impose discipline.

The oath

In addition to these three areas, there were others with a greater, or lesser, impact on the Olympic Games of Antiquity. For example, athletes, trainers, judges, relatives, friends, *aliptas* (slaves who anointed the athletes) and *alitas* (guards) had to take a solemn oath before an imposing statue of Zeus, the "Sovereign of Olympus", and "Oath-God", and over the palpitating flesh of the pig were offered to him as a burnt offering. According to Pausanias, the oath had the following text: "*Beside this image it is the custom that athletes, their fathers, brothers, and their trainers, swear an oath upon the pieces of pig flesh, that in nothing will they sin against the Olympic Games.*" The athletes also took an additional oath that they had complied strictly with the training regulations for ten successive months. And that they will not have recourse to magical or unfair procedures. An oath is also taken by those who examine the boys, and horses, involves in races, that they will decide fairly, not take bribes, and that they will keep secret at matters they learn about candidates secret, whether accepted or not.

The taking of the Oath was similar to a formal initial acceptance or incorporation procedure regarding not only sport-related issues but also ethical, and deontological issues, by which sports actors submitted to the applicable rules, on pain of perjury.

In Greece, oaths served to consolidate and strengthen contractual commitments, as a more intensive and effective form of self-commitment, and were made before witnesses, as a guarantee, and involved subjection to divine authority, if the oath was violated. Perhaps the most famous oath, which is still made by all physicians, is the Hippocratic Oath.

Although Pierre de Coubertin, the founder of the Olympic Games of the Modern Age, had a law degree,[60] he opposed the profusion of rules in the revived Olympic Games.[61] However, Coubertin nevertheless included an oath at the Olympic Games, as from the Antwerp Games in 1920. The oath, which was written by Coubertin himself, was as follows: *"In the name of all competitors, I promise that we shall take part in these Olympic Games, respecting and abiding by the rules that govern them, in the true spirit of sportsmanship, for the glory of sport and the honour of our teams."*

At the 2020 Tokyo Olympic Games, which took place in 2021, because of the postponement of the Games due to COVID-19, the oath, which was taken by athletes, trainers and umpires at the opening ceremony, was altered, by adding the words "*inclusion*" and "*equality*", which resulted in the following text: "*We promise to take part in these Olympic Games, respecting and abiding by the rules and in the spirit of fair play, inclusion and equality. Together we stand in solidarity and commit ourselves to sport without doping, without cheating, without any form of discrimination. We do this for the honour of our teams, in respect for the Fundamental Principles of Olympism, and to make the world a better place through sport.*"[62]

The penalties system

As Eduardo Gamero CASADO[63] acknowledges, the sport penalties system has existed since antiquity, although it has suffered "*radical transformations*". The truth is that there was already a disciplinary, at that time, which ensured due compliance with the rules, and punished breaches of the rules as previously enumerated, which is yet another indication of the existence of a sport law at the Games of Olympia. The said oath taken by the various sports actors was precisely the means by which they submitted to the disciplinary power of the hellanoidikai.

A series of different types of penalties was listed, in accordance with the principle of typicity, which included financial, sports, political and corporal penalties, which were ranked, or scaled, from minor to very serious, according, to seriousness.

The most common **financial penalties** were fines for infringement of the rules of games and for acts of corruption. The **sport penalties** included the disqualification of the athlete, which was imposed in cases of brutality, or ignoble conduct.

Political penalties, which were less common, included a ban on participation in the next Games, which was imposed for violations of the Olympic Truce. The sources differ regarding the number of violations of the Olympic Truce. There are records of violations in 480 BCE (75th Olympiad), 476 BCE (76th Olympiad), 420 BCE (90th Olympiad), 404 BCE (94th Olympiad) and 363 BCE (104th Olympiad). Exclusion from the Games included the obligation to pay a fine, and reputational consequences, that is, stigmatisation.

Indeed, violators of the Olympic Truce were disrespected, and disregarded forever and by all, via humiliating forms of ostracisation. This was because violation of the Truce was considered to be sacrilege, which rendered the offender impure, a dangerous citizen, who had violated the sacred law and had therefore made a malediction deserving of divine punishment, which led to remorse and to the disapproval of other believers. It is noted that the Olympic Truce was associated with a judicial truce. Some records indicate that the courts were closed during the Truce, so that judgements could not be enforced, sentences could not be implemented and goods could not be seized. More importantly, the death penalty could not be imposed or executed during the Truce.

This left **corporal punishment**, which involved the whipping of athletes, that is, flagellation, or beating with a rod, which was a form of punishment commonly imposed on slaves under the general law. Such penalties were, for example, imposed on athletes from cities that were temporarily or permanently excluded from the Games,[64] who gave false information regarding their origin, in order to be able to compete (these city-based bans could amount to life bans), and meant that even spectators from those cities could not attend the Games. There are also records of corporal punishment of athletes, who tried to bribe judges.

Athletes who failed to appear for the events for which they were registered were also penalised, if their explanations were not accepted. The paradigmatic example of this is the case of Theagenes of Thaos, who was fined because, being registered to compete in both the boxing event and the pankration, withdrew from the second event, because he was exhausted after participating in the boxing event. The athlete, Serapion, a pankratiast, was penalised at the 201st Olympiad, for failure to appear for the event. This was classed as an act of cowardice because he ran away on the eve of the event, for fear of his rival.

Here too, the oath also played a crucial role as an expression of sport actors' submission to the repressive and coercive nature of the various Olympic Laws. The oath functioned as a mechanism by which sports actors demonstrated their knowledge of, and subjection to, the coercive nature of the rules, in the way that Aristotle described in his famous work *The Nicomachean Ethics*, according to which evil people must be punished with pain, and punishment must be as contrary as possible to the persons preferred pleasures, that is, that the fear of the punishment, or penalty, is the most effective way to enforce the Law.

The enforceable nature of the rules was therefore unquestionable and arose even before the Games had started, that is, in the Olympic Truce. For, as René BONDOUX stresses, "*The fundamental law of sport is that of the friendship and understanding that unites athletes, not only within cities, but also between different cities, notwithstanding their rivalries. This can also explain the truce that was imposed on warriors while the Games were ongoing. In those days, athletes complied with severe regulations, which instituted penalties and forbid sport offences, which had such an enforceability that no city, and therefore no athlete, wherever he was from, challenged.*"[65]

The deterrent nature of the sanctions, combined with the shame that came with the violation of sacred rules, and the importance placed on the honour and ethics of the athletes, is perhaps the reason why it was not necessary to impose many penalties, throughout the 1200-year duration of the Olympic Games.

"Sport justice" at the Olympic Games of Antiquity

The hellanoidikai were responsible for the exercise of disciplinary power during the various events at the Olympic Games of Antiquity.

A right of appeal lies from the decisions of the hellanoidikai to the Olympic Council, or Senate,[66] which was the supreme body responsible for the management of the Games. The magistrates, who comprised that body, were elected for each Olympiad and were called the *mastroi*.

It was therefore established, at that time, that anyone, who did not accept all or part of a decision, could challenge it. However, all decisions regarding technical issues arising in the competition itself could never be annulled, which meant, for example, that the result of an event could not be altered, even if it had been achieved by means contrary to the applicable rules.

All that was possible in such circumstances was to punish the offenders. It was fundamentally from this that the current and no less controversial principle of the authority of the referee, that is, the so-called field of play doctrine, according to which the referee (expert) error in the application of a technical rule does result in the repetition of a game, because there can be no re-refereeing. Such errors are functional, and can only be reversed if and when identified during the event, no distinction was even made at that time between errors of fact and errors of law. Referees must apply the rules of the game, but the facts he takes into consideration cannot be disputed, in the name of legal certainty as a legal asset, and in defence of the intangibility of the rules of the game.

However, it is relevant that the hellanoidikai could be held liable for their erroneous or negligent decisions. For, despite the fact that they were assumed to be impartial, of irreprehensible conduct, and of undisputable probity, to the extent that Pindarus called Olympia the "*Queen of Truth*", the hellanoidikai were nevertheless subject to criticism, and to condemnation, because of their erroneous, or negligent, decisions. The paradigmatic case was that of the athlete Eupolemus, of Elis, who, in 396 BCE (96th Olympiad) won the stadion, according to two hellanoidikai. This was disputed by the third and final hellanoidikon, who considered that the event had been won by Leon of Ambracia. Leon of Ambracia appealed to the Olympic Council, or Senate, which decided in his favour. However, the victory awarded to Eupolemus stood, because it was not possible to reverse the sports decisions of the hellanoidikai.

The publicising of rules, penalties and results

As already mentioned, the Greeks were careful to reduce the rules to writing and did not rely on oral tradition, in order to ensure that all citizens addressed by the rules knew what they were. The Olympic Laws were engraved in detail in bronze, in a public and visible location, to be available for consultation by a broad group of people, which was also a source of increased collective authority.

The Greeks also adopted the same approach to the publicising of penalties, with a view to the transparency and publicising thereof. This approach was also intended to shame the offender, by describing the rule violation committed, and the penalty imposed for it, which not only generated repulsion amongst the populace but also served an educational purpose, that is, it made other athletes, and the citizenry, in general, aware of the duty of strict compliance with the law. The publicising of penalties and the reasons why they were imposed permitted full exercise of the right of defence by those who wanted to challenge the decision. The fundamental aim of this, in line with what is now enshrined in Article 10 of the Universal Declaration of Human Rights, was to defend the interests of justice.

The hellanoidikai also recorded the results achieved in the various events, in a historical record, which, although not used to compare records, an idea that did not exist at that time, was another example of the sharing of information and knowledge with the entire populace, and of the recognition and glorification of the winners. However, it was also evidence of the Greek concerns regarding transparency and voluntary subjection to public scrutiny, which is typical of those who act with impartiality and objectivity and in a non-arbitrary and non-discretionary manner.

The emergence of a sports protocol at Olympia

Sport events, *particularly* mega-events, of which the Olympic Games of the Modern Age are the ultimate example, involve a series of rules and traditions, plus the social and institutional acts that surround them, which are not strictly sporting in nature, and involve a series of protocolary acts. For example, the opening and closing ceremonies, receptions, press conferences, and award ceremonies. Protocol is increasingly important, and Olympic Protocol is so important that it merits an entire chapter of the Olympic Charter, and an IOC Protocol Guide, which covers the protocol applicable to all locations and spaces for which the Organising Committee of the Olympic Games is responsible.

This all started at the Olympic Games of Antiquity. Although the event was initially a one-day event, its solemnity and ceremonial aspect became more important, as its duration grew. Two days before the festival began, the procession of judges, priests and athletes, the latter accompanied by their fathers, brothers and trainers, with horses and chariots, from Elis to Olympia, a 57-km procession, which was surrounded by solemnity, rites and much aesthetics, and had standardised procedures and protocols. The ceremonies began with the registration of the athletes and the official oath, all of which were duly prepared. In those days, there was an opening ceremony and a closing ceremony, both of which are now expressly referred to in the Olympic Charter. The closing ceremony took place on the fifth and final day, and involved rituals, some of which are enacted to this day. These rituals included the ritual of the Olympic fire, the lighting of the Olympic lamp, processions, sacrifices, expressions of gratitude to the Gods, award of prizes, congratulations of the winners, who went up to the altars, thanked Zeus for their triumphs, and the holding of banquets for the winners. There were also festivities organised by the city delegations, songs, hymns, vows and other moments, all planned out in detail, with much pomp, circumstance and symbolism. In the evening, there was an arts festival. There was little room for improvisation.

It is noteworthy that, as today, there were places of honour at the event locations, particularly in the stadium, where the magistrates, priests, the deputies of the polis, numerous officials, civil and religious employees, prominent generals, foreign ambassadors, other high dignitaries, citizens and benefactors of the city, were seated, all in accordance with an order of precedence, just like current state and sport protocols.

The role of law in the decision to terminate the Olympic Games of Antiquity

Most records[67] indicate that the Olympic Games of Antiquity were banned in 393 CE by an edict of the Roman Emperor Theodosius I, which proclaimed Christianity as an official religion, and viewed the Olympic Games as a source of paganism, and therefore as something that to be prohibited.

It is therefore concluded that Law played a role in the end of the Olympic Games of Antiquity, just as it did in their beginning.

Conclusion: the Olympic Games of Antiquity were the cradle of modern sport law

We shall now summarise our arguments and formulate our conclusions. Accordingly,

7.1. The Olympic Games of Antiquity were born in 776 BCE at Olympia. The Olympic Truce Treaty was made in order to facilitate the Games. Law also laid down equal training conditions prior to the Games training, and for the registration of athletes.

7.2. The Games complied with their own specific organisational schema, which involved a multiplicity of persons, primarily the athletes, trainers, and the umpires/judges, the hellanoidikai, who had a variety of different tasks, which included the application of the Fundamental Laws of Olympia, of which there were three hierarchically ranked types, that is, the Olympic Laws, the Olympic Regulations and the Event Rules. The eligibility rules played a clearly preponderant role in this acquis.

7.3. The various actors accepted this common body of rules (essentially in written form, but with strong roots in Natural Law) as binding on them, by taking the oath, and by submitting to the imposition of a variety of penalties, that is, sport, financial, political and corporal penalties. A right of appeal against these penalties lay to the Olympic Council, or Senate, in the context of a genuine "sport justice" which ensured the right of those found guilty of sport offences to contest all or part of decisions, with which did not agree. Additionally these authority of the hellanoidikai was safeguarded, as their sport decisions could not be reversed, despite the fact that these "supreme judges of the Greeks" could be held liable for incorrect decisions, as did indeed occur.

7.4. The preservation of sport ethics was already a priority at the Olympic Games of Antiquity. Doping already existed, but was not typified, as it did not merit any ethical or legal censure, despite the existence of various practices that could today be considered to amount to prohibited methods. Endogenous violence, that is, violence in sport, and exogenous violence, that is, violence associated with sport, were already dealt with in the rules, as was corruption. There are various records of the imposition of severe penalties for such offences. Concerns regarding the avoidance of conflicts of interest and the assurance of transparency led to the institution of rules that prohibited the simultaneous occupation of positions that might lead to conflicts of interest, among other salutary concerns, which explain the publicising of rules, penalties and the results achieved at the Olympic Games of Antiquity, many centuries before Codes of Ethics or Conduct were developed for sport actors.

7.5. The relationship between Law and the Olympic Games of Antiquity is also based on realities that existed at the time, which were also present in the world of sport, such as policing and protocol.

7.6. Most historical records indicate that the Olympic Games of Antiquity were also ended by a legal instrument, that is, the edict of Emperor Theodosius I. As the Roman period evolved and with the flourishing of Roman Law, which was also applied to sport, there followed one of many stages during which rules and sport intermingle, as is inevitably the case, when the context is a competition. There can be no sport competition without various types of rules. The Olympic Games, the first true sports competitions in the History of Humanity, are proof of this.

7.7. In the final decades of the 20th century, sport law emerged as an autonomous branch of law, and various authors, especially the Italian GIANNINI, recognised the existence of a sport legal order. Greek law was obviously not systematic, and this is reflected in the Olympic rules. It is also clear that the private sources of law that now exist did not exist then, so that the Olympic Laws were fundamentally public law instruments. There are other obvious natural differences between the Greek event at Olympia and the truly planetary Modern Olympic Games, and these differences are obviously reflected in the regulatory structure governing events, which are paralleled in the continental and world championships of the various sports.

7.8. Nevertheless, we consider, and have therefore sought to demonstrate in this chapter, that the source of contemporary sport law, which is more than just Olympic Law, was born at Olympia, and that the modern sport legal order, as defined by GIANNINI, with the constitutive elements he listed, that is, (i) the existence of a multiplicity of individual or juridical persons; (ii) the existence of an autonomous organisational structure, that is, the idea of a system, of an ordered, articulated, self-organised whole and (iii) the existence of a regulatory corpus, an acquis and a structured and coherent set of rules, with an overall logic and inherent developmental dynamic, which the said multiplicity of persons regard as binding.

Notes

1 See https://dicionario.priberam.org/desporto.

2 See Article 2 of Law 30/2004 of 21 July.

3 For this association of international, Olympic and non-Olympic federations, sport presupposes: (i) a competitive aspect; (ii) a competitive result that does not depend on luck; (iii) the health of the athletes not being placed at risk; (iv) not causing harm to other living beings and (v) the absence of a monopoly regarding sports equipment. This definition is based on a subdivision of sport into five types: (i) predominantly physical activities; (ii) predominantly mental activities; (iii) predominantly motorised activities; (iv) activities that predominantly involve coordination and (v) activities that predominantly involve animals – See Javier Rodríguez TEN, *Los e-Sports como desporte? Análisis jurídico y técnico-deportivo de su naturaleza y los requisitos legales exigidos*, Madrid, Editorial Reus, 2018, page 56.

4 The Portuguese state contributed to this text and has approved it.

5 See, *inter alia*, Artur FLAMÍNIO DA SILVA, *A Resolução de Conflitos Desportivos em Portugal: Entre o Direito Público e o Direito Privado*, Coimbra, Almedina, 2017, pages 43 et seq.; Jean-Michel MARMAYOU, *Etude 106 – Le sport: notion juridique*, droidusport.com, 2006.

6 There is no consensus regarding this issue in legal theory, case law or between different countries. For those who consider that physical activity and physical effort are of the essence of sport, the so-called "sports of the mind", which rely more on the intellectual capacity of the competitors, or which have a very minor physical component, should not be considered to

be sports. The following are examples of such activities: Olympic shooting, chess, draughts and bridge. Bridge is the subject of a judgement of the Court of Justice of the European Union, which held, contrary to the Conclusions of Advocate General Maciej Szpunar, that bridge is not a sport, because it has an insignificant physical component – see Judgement of 26 October 2017, Case C – 90/16, *The English Bridge Union Limited v. Commissioners for Her Majesty's Revenue & Customs*, http://curia.europa.eu/juris/liste.jsf?language=en&num=C-90/16, accessed on 13.11.2019.

7 See Diego Medina MORALES, "El deporte en la sociedad actual. Reflexiones en cuanto a su ubicación y perspectivas", *Los retos del deporte profesional y profesionalizado en la sociedad atual*, Dir. Ignacio Jiménez-Soto e J.L. Pérez-Serrabona González, Madrid, Ed. Reus, 2017, page 21.

8 See "Bases estructurales del sistema deportivo", *Fundamentos de Derecho Deportivo (Adaptado a Estudios No Jurídicos*, Madrid, Tecnos, 2012, pages 55–56.

9 See Derecho Público del Deporte, Universidad de Alicante, 1991, page 44.

10 See Frédéric BUY, Jean-Michel MARMAYOU, Didier PORACCHIA and Fabrice RIZZO, *Droit du sport*, Paris, L.G.D.J., 2006, pages 2–3.

11 Cf. *Vinculação versus Liberdade: O Processo de Constituição e Extinção da Relação Laboral do Praticante Desportiva*, Coimbra Editora, 2002, pages 19–20.

12 Cf. "Direito do Desporto", *Enciclopédia de Direito do Desporto*, Coord. Alexandre Miguel MESTRE, Coimbra, Gestlegal, 2019, page 156.

13 Cf. FREITAS DO AMARAL, Diogo, *Introdução ao Estudo do Direito*, I Vol., Coimbra, Almedina, 2004, page 337.

14 Cf. "Internormatividade desportiva e homo sportivus", *Direito do Desporto Profissional: contributos de um curso de Pós-Graduação*, Coimbra, Almedina, 2011, page 7.

15 Cf. "Os sistemas normativos do desporto", in *Estudos de Homenagem a Miguel Galvão Telles*, Compiled by Jorge MIRANDA, Gomes CANOTILHO, José de SOUSA BRITO, Miguel NOGUEIRA DE BRITO, Margarida LIMA REGO and Pedro MÚRIAS, Coimbra, Almedina, 2012, pages 286 e 290.

16 Cf. José Manuel MEIRIM (Editor), *Lei do Tribunal Arbitral do Desporto: Introdução. Referências. Notas.*, Coimbra, Almedina, 2017, pages 66–67.

17 "O impacte da 'legislação Covid' na regulamentação desportiva: que efeitos futuros na determinação da competência material do Tribunal Arbitral do Desporto?", *Revista Internacional de Arbitragem e Conciliação*, N.° 15–2021. Associação Portuguesa de Arbitragem, Coimbra, Almedina, pages 9–30.

18 *As Federações Desportivas: Contributo para o estudo do ordenamento jurídico desportivo*, Coimbra Editora, 2001, page 162.

19 See *Direito Desportivo*, Confederação Brasileira de Futebol de Salão, Fortaleza, 1983, page 11.

20 See "Bases históricas del derecho deportivo", *La Revista 'Citius, Altius, Fortius'*, Tomo X (1968), page 376.

21 Cf. "Roman Law and the Foundations of Contemporary Sports Law: The Approach of Justinian's Legislation" (January 2011) and "The Importance of Certain Roman Law Solutions for Contemporary Sports Law, 2nd FIEP European Congress" (June 2020), both available on researchgate.net.
22 Adolfo-Díaz-Bautista CREMADES and Julio César MUÑIZ PÉREZ, "La financiación del deporte en Roma. Hacia un Derecho Deportivo Romano", *E-Slegal History Review*, 24 (2017), pages 1–15.
23 See "Síntese da História do Desporto", in *Povos e Culturas- N.º 9: Cultura e Desporto*, Braga, Centro de Estudos dos Povos e Culturas de Expressão Portuguesa da Universidade Católica Portuguesa, 2005, page 152.
24 See *A Federação Desportiva como Sujeito Público do Sistema Desportivo*, Coimbra Editora, 2002, page 47, footnote 96.
25 See *Los Extranjeros y el Derecho en la Antigua Grecia*, Universidad Rey Juan Carlos Servicio de Publicaciones/Dykinson, Madrid, 2001, page 43.
26 See *La cultura giuridica dell'antica Grecia: legge, politica, giustizia*, Croci editore, Roma, 2021, page 79.
27 See *Filosofia do Direito e do Estado: Histórias e Teorias*, Coimbra, Almedina, 2020, page 78.
28 See "Lex Aquilia y El Deporte", *Revista Jurídica- Facultad de Jurisprudencia y Ciencias Sociales y Politicas*, available at www.revistajuridicaonline.com/wp-content/uploads/2004/01/17_Lex_Aquila_y_Deporte.pdf.
29 See Martinho Neves MIRANDA, *O Direito no Desporto*, 2nd Edition, Rio de Janeiro, Editora Lumen Iuris, 2011, page 82.
30 See Davida KRISTY, *Coubertin's Olympics: How the Games Began*, Minneapolis, Lerner Publications Company, 1995, page 31.
31 See Dolores FIEL VARELA, "Aproximación al régimen jurídico de la práctica deportiva en la Administración Pública Romana", *Revista General de Derecho Romano*, 26 (2006), available at www.iustel.com/v2/revistas/detalle_revista.asp?id_noticia=417676&d=1.
32 *O Desporto na ordem jurídico-constitucional brasileira*, São Paulo, Malheiros Editores Ltda, 1995, page 18.
33 One of the most famous cases of violation of this rule involved the boxer Damoxenos, who killed his adversary Creugas, by taking advantage of him when he was completely defenceless. Damoxenos claimed the victory, and the crown of laurels, but the judges disqualified him and awarded the victory to Creugas, posthumously.
34 See CAS 2014/A/3759, *Dutee Chand v. AFI & IAAF*, 24.07.2015; CAS 2018/O/5794 & 5798, *Caster Semenya v. IAAF & Athletics South Africa* v. IAAF, 30.04.2019.
35 See CAS 2018/A/1480 *Pistorius v. IAAF*, 16.05.2008 and CAS 2020/A/6807, Blake Keeper v. IAAF, 23.10.2020.
36 See *IOC Consensus Meeting on Sex Reassignment and Hyperandrogenism* – November 2015.
37 See *A Arte e os Jogos Gregos na Antiguidade: As representações das actividades físico-atléticas na cerâmica clássica grega nos períodos das figuras negras e vermelhas*, Coimbra, Almedina, 2009, page 51.

38 This is the quote: "*The Olympic Games of Ancient Greece were discriminatory. Greeks, who worked and descendants of Greeks and foreigners, women and slaves were discriminated against, in one way or other. This is why they could not compete in the Games, or, in the case of women, even watch them. The Games were only intended for Greeks, who were free, the offspring of Greek parents, and did not work. This therefore occurred when the prestige of the Games was at its highest. The practice of sports exercises was a privilege of the military and socially dominant class, or a means to impose its internal dominance, and also for the purposes of offensive and defensive war against foreigners. Non-members of the upper caste were often excluded from the gymnasiums. Those who did not travel to the Olympic Games, and others, needed sufficient financial resources, in order to cover their participation expenses. They were therefore amateurs because they were rich.*"

39 Here too, there is no consensus among legal theorists. There are records of a boxing champion, Armenius, in 388 BCE.

40 There are even a few sources that indicate that the ban only included married women.

41 There are also some records that indicate that this ban did not apply to unmarried women, who were virgins.

42 Some records indicate that this separation existed from the earliest days of the Games. Others indicate a division that only occurred from the 37th Olympiad, when minors were first permitted to compete, with the introduction of the Infantis (up to 18), Imberbes (19–20 years) and Men (over 20 years) categories.

43 Cited by José Antonio MARTINEZ VELA, *El Deporte en el Mundo Antiguo. Algunas Claves a través de las Fuentes Literarias y Patrísticas*, January 2016, text provided by the author.

44 See Magali WIÉNER, *Les Jeux Olympiques d'hier à aujourd'hui*, Paris, Éditions Flammarion, page 19.

45 See *O Desporto e as Estruturas Sociais*, Lisboa, Prelo Editora, 1967, pages 22–23.

46 See Maria Helena da ROCHA PEREIRA, *Estudos de História da Cultura Clássica I Volume – Cultura Grega*, 12.ª Edição, Coimbra, Fundação Calouste Gulbenkian, 2012, page 324.

47 For example, one of the inscriptions contains a clear moral code: "*Win with the speed of your feet, and with the strength of your body, and not with money!*"

48 See Didier VEILLON, "Triche et sport: perspective historique", *Les Cahiers du droit du sport* n.º 42, Dir. Jean-Michel MARMAYOU, 2016, page 17.

49 Conrado DURÁNTEZ, *Existiria violência nos Jogos Olímpicos da Antiguidade?*, Lisboa, Ministério da Educação, Direcção-Geral dos Desportos, Desporto e Sociedade Antologia de Textos no. 68, page 10.

50 See *Introdução ao Direito Desportivo*, Irmãos Pongetti Editores, Rio de Janeiro, 1952, page 105.

51 See *O Direito e os Desportos (Breve estudo do direito desportivo)*, Lisboa, Procural Editora, 1946, page 35.

52 Eugenia FRANCIOSI states that after the 6th century BCE, winners were entitled to the erection of a statue of them in Olympia, and refers to this as an expression of their "*image right*" – cf. *Athletae, agitatores, venatores: Aspetti del phenomenon Sportivo nella legislazione postclassica e giustinianea*, Torino, G. Giappichelli Editore, 2012, page 29.
53 Rosella FRASCA, *Saggu sulla Carta Olimpica*, Roma, Società Stama Sportiva, 2008, page 15.
54 See Delfim F. LEÃO, "Os Honorários dos Atletas Vencedores' (a propósito de Plutarco, Sol. 23.3.)", in *O Espírito Olímpico no novo milénio*, Coord. Francisco DE OLIVEIRA, Coimbra, Imprensa da Universidade, 2000, pages 77–78.
55 See Jean-Paul THUILLER, "Ils trichaient déjà", *Les Collections de l'Histoire n.° 40: Les Jeux Olympiques d'Athènes à Pékin, Juillet-Septembre 2008*, page 38.
56 See François LAFORGE, *Los Juegos Olímpicos: Todas las olimpíadas de la era moderna*, De Vecchi Ediciones, 2012, page 17.
57 Although strict, the regulation gave this discretion to the judges, which demonstrates their power. For example, at the 142nd Olympiad, the judges decided that the pankration would exceptionally precede the boxing event, in order to allow an athlete to enter these two events in good condition.
58 See Tina ZISSIMOU, *Les Jeux Olympiques dans l'Antiquité*, Edição de Autor, Glyfada, 2000, page 23.
59 See "L'encadrement juridique des Jeux Antiques", Droit & Olympisme: Contribution à l'étude juridique d'une phénomène transnational, Actes du colloque du 4 septembre 2012 Université de La Réunion – Faculté de droit et d'économie, Dir. Mathieu MAISONNEUVE, Presses Universitaires d'Aix-Marseille, 2015, page 101.
60 He studied law because of a family imposition/tradition, but he writes in his memoirs that this was a real ordeal for him – cf. Louis CALLEBAT, *Pierre de Coubertin*, Paris, Fayard, 1988, page 43.
61 According to the French Baron, "the more regulations they adopt, the more they will be constrained. Allow Olympic organisations some flexibility" – see Monique BERLIOUX, "The International Olympic Committee", *Report of the Tenth Session of the IOA at Olympia*, Athens, IOA, 1970, page 2.
62 Free translation.
63 See *Las sanciones deportivas*, Barcelona, Bosch, 2003, page 33.
64 For example, at the 74th and 75th Olympic Games (484 and 480 BCE), the athlete Astylus of Kroton declared that he was Syracusian, when he had entered the previous Olympic Games and won the stadion when registered as a Krotoan athlete. This provoked the wrath of his fellow citizens who expropriated his palace and imprisoned him. In 384 BCE, Sotades of Crete was approached by officers from Ephesus shortly before the opening of the 99th Olympiad. He was expected to be the certain winner in the wrestling, and pentathlon, which Ephesus had no chance of winning. The athlete therefore accepted the offer of a large sum, renounced his citizenship of Crete, and competed as a citizen of Ephesus, and won. When this

was discovered, he was disqualified and banished from his native island because of his disloyalty, and was stateless for the rest of his life. At the 100th Olympiad (380 BCE), the Cretan Sotadas claimed to be from Ephesus, which resulted in him being exiled by his compatriots. At the 90th Olympiad (420 BCE), Lichas, a Spartan politician and a son of Arcesilaus, pretended to be Tebanus, but was discovered and whipped. All these cases lead us to make a comparison with Rule 41 of the Olympic Charter, which states that all competitors in the Olympic Games must be nationals of the country of the National Olympic Committee that registers him/her. The text regarding the application of this rule provides that a competitor, who is also a national of another country, must allow at least three years to elapse from his/her most recent participation in the Olympic Games for that other country, before they can compete on behalf of the country of that National Olympic Committee. The purpose of this rule is not only to ensure compliance with sport ethics but also to ensure that there are real ties of geography and blood between the athlete and the country he/she represents.

65 See René BONDOUX, *O Direito e o Desporto*, Lisboa, Edição Ministério da Educação e Cultura, 1986, page 13.

66 The Olympic Council or Senate also administered the funds in the Treasury of Zeus, which was fed by the tributes paid by all participating cities. In addition to the Public Treasury, the Games were also financed by military aid, tributes paid by defeated enemies, land rents, pilgrims' donations and the proceeds of financial penalties.

67 There are some who argue the Games only ended in the 5th century BCE, during the reign of Theodosius II (408 to 450 BCE), the grandson of Theodosius I. See Caillan DAVONPORT, "Mythbushing Ancient Rome: Did Christians Ban the Ancient Olympics?", available at Mythbusting Ancient Rome: Did Christians Ban the Ancient Olympics? | Ancient Origins (ancient-origins.net).

2 Olympic Charter

The sports law instrument driving a universal fight for (Sports) Ethics

Sports Ethics at the centre of the universal fundamental principles and missions of the International Olympic Committee

The International Olympic Committee ("IOC"), in the Olympic Charter ("OC"), is clear and emphatic in the way it stresses the importance of Sports Ethics, from the outset, by establishing *"respect for universal fundamental ethical principles"*, as one of the *"Fundamental Principles of Olympism"*.[1] This dispels any doubt that Sports Ethics is rightly one of the IOC's priorities. One of the IOC's fundamental roles is therefore to *"encourage and support the promotion of ethics and good governance in sport"*.[2]

Consistently, the OC[3] also provides that the IOC also has a mission to "*protect clean athletes and the integrity of sport by leading the fight against doping and by taking action against all forms of competition manipulation and related corruption*" – which shows the IOC's determination to combat the scourges that jeopardise integrity in sport. After the first, positive approach, that is, the existence of fundamental ethical principles, the IOC also has an enforcement role, that is, the fight against the violation of these principles.

The eighth mission attributed to the IOC in the OC is to "*promote safe sport and the protection of athletes against all forms of harassment and abuse*". Harassment and abuse in sport are unfortunately a phenomenon that has recently become more widely known in sport, that is, moral/sexual harassment, and abuse, which is primarily sexual. The eighth mission therefore involves a positive approach, that is, the promotion of safe sport and the protection of athletes (to protect their physical and mental integrity) and a negative approach, which recognises the existence of other scourges that also need to be eradicated, or at least mitigated.

It is therefore within this framework of mission and obligation to act that the IOC prioritises the promotion and guarantee of Sports Ethics.

DOI: 10.4324/9781003569749-3

The IOC's legal strategy for pursuing its missions in the context of Sports Ethics

The choice of the Olympic Charter as the fundamental legal instrument

According to the Introduction of the OC its purpose *"is the codification of the fundamental principles of Olympism, and the rules and by-laws adopted by the IOC. It governs the organisation, action and functioning of the OM and establishes the conditions for the celebration of the Olympic Games."* This text and the entire text of the OC suggest that the legislator's aim is to create a "Scriptures" or a Codex of Olympism, via meticulous normative filtering and methodical structuring of the organisation of the Olympic Movement.[4]

The Introduction of the OC outlines the OC and identifies the three main purposes of the OC, that is, (i) *The Olympic Charter, as a basic constitutional instrument, and recalls the Fundamental Principles and essential values of Olympism;* (ii) *to serve as statutes for the International Olympic Committee* and (iii) defines *"the main reciprocal rights and obligations of the three main constituents of the Olympic Movement, namely the International Olympic Committee, the International Federations and the National Olympic Committees, as well as the Organising Committees for the Olympic Games (OCOG)".*

The text of these three purposes and their interpretation lead us to see parallels between the OC and other more familiar legal texts. On the one hand, the OC is similar to a constitution, as it is the basic fundamental document of the Olympic Movement, whose ultimate purpose is to stand as the supreme law of its corresponding legal order (*lex superior, lex maxima* or "fundamental law"), which, in a complex and complete way, binds all within the universe of sport. Other similarities with a constitution lie in the fact that the OC is foundational, founding or constitutive, and establishes a set of principles and fundamental values that govern a particular model of organisation, that is, the organisation of world sport, and seeks to give stability and permanence to the order it governs. On the other hand, the OC is similar to a contract, because it is an act that governs the internal organisation of the IOC, the OC constitutes or encompasses within it the IOC Statutes. Finally, by defining the rights and obligations of the components of the Olympic Movement, the OC is akin to a contract. The OC is a composite legal text that combines general principles with more technical rules, which includes both enforcement provisions and mere rules of behaviour. Similarly, the OC combines typical public law rules, such as the rules about exclusive competence to represent a country, with rules typical of relations between private individuals, such as the concept of "ownership" of the Olympic Games.

Despite everything referred to earlier, that is, the fact that the OC is the highest expression of the Olympic Movement and rests on principles of supposedly universal legal value, the OC is a document approved by the IOC, which is a legal person created under and governed by Swiss private law. The IOC has the legitimacy to adopt its own rules, but this right does not derive from a higher legal order that grants it this legitimacy. It therefore makes sense to question the legal form and basis of the power of the IOC to enforce the OC, by imposing it on all bodies that voluntarily become members of the Olympic Movement and are therefore addressed by the OC.

If, in the eyes of the IOC and the Olympic Movement as a whole, the OC has the guise of a genuine international treaty that does not correspond to the legal nature of the text, because the IOC has no basis in an international convention and its members do not represent governments.

It could be considered that the OC claims and has universal legal value, not because of its legal nature but rather because of a moral authority, or extra-legal element, namely the social, economic and sporting impact of the Olympic Games. The basis of the externally binding nature of the OC lies precisely in the commitment to and voluntary recognition of it by those addressed by it, that is, a diverse community of natural and legal persons, be they states, NOCs, international sports federations or others. The OC therefore has legal supremacy, not because of its legal enforceability but because of custom, and because of the socio-economic transcendence of the Olympic Games.[5] This does not, of course, mean that it is a perfect text – either because of the contradictions between its own different Rules or because, as identified in different parts of this book, it sometimes adopts solutions that seem to go against human and fundamental rights.

Now that we know the nature and scope of the OC, we can have a better understanding of the matters we highlighted in this chapter, namely that the IOC, despite being (merely) a Swiss private law association, a non-governmental organisation, is able, via the OC, to compel a plethora of public and private actors, to collaborate with the IOC in its mission within the framework of Sports Ethics. The purpose of this text is therefore simply to draw attention to how a global/universal fight for Sports Ethics can be implemented, both geographically and personally, that is, in relation to those addressed by the rules issued by the IOC, under the OC.

The adoption of, and reference to, other legal sources in the Olympic Charter itself, or to complement it

Since the OC is the central and fundamental legal instrument through which the IOC pursues its mission, it complements it with other sources, particularly the Code of Ethics, which is an integral part of the OC and is therefore included in any legal or contractual reference to subjection to the OC.

As with the Code of Ethics, the IOC particularly adopts and refers to the following complementary legal instruments, the main ones being the World Anti-Doping Code and the Olympic Movement Code on the Prevention of the Manipulation of Competitions.

The creation of the IOC Ethics Commission

Being aware that the enforcement of legal sources requires an appropriate institutional solution, the second step taken by the IOC in its legal strategy involves the creation, within its internal organisation, of a body dedicated to the issue.

Accordingly, and acting within its power to establish Commissions, which have an advisory role in relation to the IOC Session, the Executive Board or the IOC President, the IOC[6] lists seven Commissions, the second of which is "Ethics Commission".[7] The Ethics Commission is the only one of the seven Commissions with a rule[8] devoted to it, which indicates its importance. Thus, according to the OC, *"The IOC Ethics Commission is charged with defining and updating a framework of ethical principles, including a Code of Ethics, based upon the values and principles enshrined in the Olympic Charter of which the said Code forms an integral part. In addition, it investigates complaints raised in relation to the non-respect of such ethical principles, including breaches of the Code of Ethics and, if necessary, proposes sanctions to the IOC Executive Board.* "

The legal strategy for a universal personal scope of application

The Code of Ethics binds "all participants in the Olympic Games", and all "Olympic Parties"

The IOC Code of Ethics is an integral part of the OC and applies to *"all participants in the Olympic Games"*.[9] By defining those addressed by the OC in this way, the IOC ensures that none of the actors who want to enter and participate in the Olympic Games can do so without complying with the required ethical conditions. While the legislative method sometimes involves a generic identification of those addressed, in list form, at other times,[10] perhaps to dispel any doubts, the IOC is more specific and specifically identifies those addressed by the Code, stating from the outset that the Code binds not only the IOC itself (and its members and administration) in their duty to comply with the Olympic Charter (its Fundamental Principles, and particularly the Olympic ideal inspired by Pierre de Coubertin) but also the following other *"Olympic Parties"*: (i) the National Olympic Committees (NOCs); (ii) the international sports federations; (iii) the *"Stakeholders"* in the *"Continuous and/or Targeted Dialogue"* for the election of the host city of future Olympic Games and Youth Olympic Games; (iv) Organising Committees of the Olympic Games and (v) participants in the Olympic Games and the "Recognised Organisations" (the "Olympic Parties").

The obligations imposed on "Sports Organisations" in general

a) The IOC requires *"Sports Organisations"* in general to

    (i) Include rules about compliance with the Olympic Charter and the IOC Code of Ethics, including the World Anti-Doping Code and the

Code of the Olympic Movement on the Prevention of the Manipulation of Results, in their Statutes[11];

(ii) Adopt ethical principles and rules, under the IOC Code of Ethics, from the bottom to the top of the organisation, with a designated individual within the organisation (e.g. the Compliance officer) responsible for implementing these principles and rules[12];

(iii) Establish an Ethics Commission with a defined mission, which includes members independent of the governing bodies[13];

(iv) Adopt and publish a conflicts of interest policy that prohibits all actual, potential and/or perceived conflicts of interest[14];

(v) Adopt and publish a conflicts of interest policy that prohibits any current, potential and/or perceived conflicts of interest[15];

(vi) Adopt open and transparent procurement procedures for commercial contracts and tenders (other than in the context of events)[16];

(vii) Adopt a zero-tolerance policy in the fight against doping in sport, undertaking an anti-doping policy and adopting anti-doping regulations under the World Anti-Doping Code. Anti-doping programmes must also be independent and free of any real or perceived conflicts of interest, namely via the creation of a National Anti-Doping Organisation (NADO) independent of sports bodies and anti-doping laboratories. International federations are advised to delegate anti-doping programmes to the International Testing Agency (ITA);

(viii) Adopt a zero-tolerance policy in the fight against competition manipulation at all levels, and ensure that their regulations comply with the Olympic Movement Code on the Prevention of the Manipulation of Competitions;

(ix) Protect athletes, their support staff and officials from the risk of competition manipulation through robust prevention and educational programmes[17];

(x) Adopt a zero-tolerance policy regarding violations of safeguard principles, at all levels[18];

(xi) To have a confidential internal mechanism for reporting any violation of the organisation's regulations[19];

(xii) To provide all their members (including members of the Executive) with educational and training tools regarding ethics, integrity, good governance, prevention of doping, manipulation of results, harassment and abuse[20];

(xiii) Adopt accounting principles in the preparation of their financial reports[21];

(xiv) Establish and publish, in line with sports development objectives, a clear and transparent process for allocating financial income[22];

(xv) Encourage harmonious relations and constructive partnerships with each other, with governmental and non-governmental organisations, in the interests of sport and to help sports organisations pursue their mission, provided that the principle of autonomy is respected and on condition that sports organisations do not associate themselves with any activity that could conflict with the OC.[23]

The obligations imposed on "non-governmental organisations related to sport"

The OC provides that the IOC may recognise *"non-governmental sport-related organisations"* that are active at international level, provided that their statutes and activities comply with the OC.[24]

The obligations imposed on "International Sports Federations"

The OC stipulates that the conduct of *"International Sports Federations"* must comply with the rules in the OC,[25] and therefore with its provisions regarding Sports Ethics.

The obligations imposed on "Associations of International Sports Federations", "Associations of National Olympic Committees" and "Other recognised associations and organisations"

The IOC Code of Ethics provides that its scope may be extended to cover "Associations of International Sports Federations", "Associations of National Olympic Committees" and "Other recognised associations and organisations" if they apply in writing to the IOC Ethics Commission.[26]

The obligations imposed on "National Sports Federations"

As for the "National Sports Federations", and according to the CO:

(i) One of their missions is to *"contribute to the achievement of the objectives set out in the Olympic Charter"*[27];
(ii) In order to be recognised by an NOC and be accepted as a member of an NOC, a national federation must comply with all aspects of the OC,[28] and therefore with its provisions regarding Sports Ethics.

The obligations imposed on "National Olympic Committees"

Regarding the "National Olympic Committees", the OC:

(i) Provides that the IOC only recognises entities that comply with the CO, as NOCs and associations of NOCs[29];

(ii) Stresses that the mission of the NOCs is to develop, promote and protect the Olympic Movement in their respective countries, under the OC[30];

(iii) Delimits the role of NOCs as *"to promote the fundamental principles and values of Olympism in their Countries"*[31]; *"to ensure compliance with the Olympic Charter in their Countries"*[32]; *"to act against any form of discrimination and violence in sport"*[33]; *"to adopt and implement the World Anti-Doping Code"*[34] and *"to implement the Olympic Movement Code on the Prevention of the Manipulation of Competitions"*[35];

(iv) Provides that NOCs may not, in the prosecution of their mission, be associated with any activity contrary to the OC[36];

(v) Subjects them to a duty to preserve their autonomy and to resist all pressures, particularly political, legal, religious or economic pressures that could prevent them from complying with the OC[37];

(vi) Entitles them to send competitors, team officials and other team personnel to the Olympic Games in compliance with the OC[38];

(vii) Provides that, in addition to the measures and sanctions provided regarding violation of the OC, the IOC Executive Board may take decisions to protect the Olympic Movement in the country of an NOC, including the suspension, or withdrawal of recognition of the corresponding NOC[39];

(viii) Requires the prior approval of the Statutes of the NOC by the IOC Executive Board, which approval is subject to compliance with the OC, at all times.[40]

The obligations imposed on "National Governments"

Regarding "*National Governments*", the OC stipulates that the national government of the country of any candidature must submit to the IOC a legally binding instrument in which it undertakes and guarantees that the country and its public authorities will comply with and respect the OC,[41] that is, the government and parliament of the country whose city wins the right to host Olympic Games must introduce and/or repeal the legislation necessary to make the Olympic Games viable, particularly in Sports Ethics.

The obligations imposed on the "Organising Committees of the Olympic Games (OCOG)"

Regarding the "*Organising Committees of the Olympic Games (OCOG)*", the OC essentially requires:

(i) That the OCOG must, from its establishment to its dissolution, conduct its activities under the OC, under the agreement between the IOC, the NOC and the host city, as well as under other regulations, or instructions, of the IOC Executive Board[42];

(ii) That, to be valid, all contracts concluded by the NOC regarding aspect of advertising, including the right, or licence, to use the emblem or mascot of the Olympic Games, must comply with the OC.[43]

Obligations imposed on the "Organising Committees of an IOC Session or an Olympic Congress"

Regarding the *"Organising Committees of an IOC Session or an Olympic Congress"*, the OC requires that, to be valid, contracts concluded by the organising committee of an IOC Session, or an Olympic Congress, regarding any aspect of advertising, including the right or licence to use the emblem or mascot of the Olympic Games, must comply with the OC,[44] and therefore with the Code of Ethics.

Obligations imposed on "Broadcasters, Sponsors, Partners and Other Supporters"

Regarding *"Broadcasters, Sponsors, Partners and Other Supporters"*, the OC provides that, in order to preserve the integrity and neutrality of candidature procedures, the support and promotion of any candidatures by broadcasters, sponsors, partners and other supporters, must be in a manner consistent with the rules of sport and the principles defined in the OC and the Code of Ethics.[45]

Obligations imposed on the media

The OC refers to the *"Media"* and provides that Stakeholders must not organise, or underwrite, the costs of any work by international media representatives.[46]

Obligations imposed on "Consultants"

In various sources, the IOC refers to "Consultants", and imposes the following regarding them:

(i) Consultants working with "Stakeholders" must register with the IOC's "Register of Consultants", and the NOC must monitor this registration procedure;
(ii) Consultants working for cities bidding to host the Olympic Games must register, either individually or through a company, and undertake to comply with the IOC's ethical principles, the Olympic Charter, the IOC Code of Ethics and the corresponding implementation rules, particularly the "Conflict of Interest Rules"[47];

(iii) All Consultants wishing to participate in or support a Host City project must register in the "IOC Register of Consultants in the list of NOC Stakeholders"[48];

(iv) Before providing services to any potential Host Cities, consultants (whether individual or corporate) must submit a written declaration to the IOC Chief Ethics and Compliance Officer, in which they confirm that they will comply with the ethical principles of the IOC, the OC, and the IOC Code of Ethics and its Implementation Rules, particularly the "Conflict of Interest Rules".[49]

The obligations imposed on "Olympic host cities" *(and on the corresponding NOCs) and on host city candidates*

The "Rules of Conduct for Ongoing Dialogue with Third Parties" are guided by the core principle of the Olympic value of fair play, the OC, and the IOC Code of Ethics and their implementing rules, particularly the "Rules Concerning Conflicts of Interest Affecting the Behaviour of Olympic Parties".[50] These rules apply during the host city selection procedure conducted by the IOC and must be complied with by potential Host Cities and their NOCs, as well as by all representatives of the Olympic Movement.[51]

The specific focus on the fight against doping and competition manipulation

The IOC's legal strategy also involves a focus on two scourges that undermine the reputation, veracity, transparency and integrity of sport: doping and competition manipulation. The IOC stipulates the following in a forceful corpus of complementary rules:

(i) In order to participate in the Olympic Games, competitors, team officials and other team staff must respect and comply with the OC, the World Anti-Doping Code and the Olympic Movement Code on the Prevention of the Manipulation of Competitions[52];

(ii) Compliance with the World Anti-Doping Code and the Olympic Movement Code on the Prevention of the Manipulation of Competitions is mandatory for the entire Olympic Movement[53];

(iii) All competitors in the Olympic Games, in any capacity, must comply with the rules in the OC, the World Anti-Doping Code and the Olympic Movement Code on the Prevention of the Manipulation of Competitions, as a condition precedent to their participation in the Olympic Games[54];

(iv) All participants in the Olympic Games, in any capacity, must comply with the entry procedure prescribed by the IOC Executive Board, including the signing of an entry form, which includes the obligation to comply with the OC, the World Anti-Doping Code and the Olympic Movement Code on the Prevention of Manipulation of Competition[55];

(v) Only sports that comply with the OC, the World Anti-Doping Code and the Olympic Movement Code on the Prevention of the Manipulation of Competitions are eligible for inclusion in the Olympic Games Programme[56];

(vi) The IOC Session has the power to remove any sport from the Olympic Programme, at any time, at its sole discretion, if the international sports federation that governs that sport fails to follow the OC, the World Anti-Doping Code and the Olympic Movement Code on the Prevention of the Manipulation of Competitions, or acts in a way that undermines the reputation of the Olympic Movement.[57]

Monitoring the Olympic Charter and applying sanctions to offenders

The IOC Executive Board monitors compliance with the OC and is responsible for the adoption of all IOC decisions and regulations necessary to ensure the correct implementation of the OC.[58] The IOC Ethics Commission recommends measures or sanctions to be adopted under Rule 59 of the OC, or other appropriate measures, to the IOC Executive Board, particularly those provided in the Rules for the Application of the IOC Code of Ethics.[59]

Rule 59 of the OC is a relevant provision in order to understand the number and nature of the sanctions that can be applied, in general, and regarding breaches of Sports Ethics in particular, and therefore better understand the power of the IOC to enforce the rules. It is really relevant since it applies to a wide range of parties, specifically identified. In the context of the Olympic Movement, (i) to IOC members, the Honorary President, honorary members and honour members; (ii) to International Federations; (iii) to Associations of International Federations; (iv) to National Olympic Committees; (v) to Associations of National Olympic Committees; (vi) to host cities, Organizing Committees of the Olympic Games and National Olympic Committees; (vii) to interested hosts or candidates and National Olympic Committees and (viii) to other recognised associations and organisations. In the context of the Olympic Games, Individual competitors and teams, officials, managers of any delegation as well as referees and members of the jury are also subject to measures and sanctions.

Conclusion

Because of all these, we can conclude that the IOC, based on the OC (and related legal instruments), in which Sports Ethics feature as a primary mission, has developed a legal strategy that enables it to pursue a universal policy in this area, both geographically, via a policy with global reach, and in terms of the parties bound by the policy and the related rules (on pain of the imposition of disciplinary sanctions of various types, which are sufficiently dissuasive). This is perhaps the greatest sign of the success and effectiveness of this strategy, that is, the obligation of a wide range of private bodies, that is, National Olympic Committees; national and international sports federations; Associations of International Sports Federations/Associations of National Olympic Committees/Other recognised associations and organisations; Organising Committees of Olympic Games and Organising Committees of an IOC Session or an Olympic Congress; Broadcasters, Sponsors, Partners and other Supporters; Media and Consultants, must comply with various rules in Sports Ethics, and public bodies, such as national governments and host cities or candidates to host the Olympic Games, despite the private nature of the IOC.

The IOC's role in pursuing its mission also includes the work done by its Ethics Commission and its special focus on the fight against doping and the competition manipulation, anchored in its own Codes.

It can therefore be concluded that the OC is undoubtedly the sports law instrument that drives a universal fight for (Sports) Ethics.

Notes

1 Fundamental Principle 1 of the OC.
2 Rule 2.1 of the OC.
3 Rule 2.9 of the OC.
4 Jean Pierre KARAQUILLO, *Le droit du sport*, 2nd Édition, Paris, Dalloz, 1997, page 8.
5 Alexandre Miguel MESTRE, *Direito e Jogos Olímpicos*, Coimbra, Almedina, 2008, page 32.
6 Rule 21 of the OC.
7 Rule regarding the Application of Rule 21, no. 2 of the OC.
8 Rule 22 of the OC.
9 Article 1 of the 'Rules regarding the application, during the Olympic Games, of Articles 7 to 10 of the IOC Code of Ethics' and the "Code of the Olympic Movement on the Prevention of Manipulation of Competitions".
10 Introduction to the IOC Code of Ethics.
11 "Universal Basic Principles of Good Governance in the Olympic Movement – Rules for the Implementation of the IOC Code of Ethics, Principle 2 – Institutional Governance".
12 Principle 3 – Ethical Standards and Integrity, 3.1. Ethical Principles.
13 Principle 3 – Ethical Standards and Integrity, 3.2. Ethics Committee.
14 Principle 3 – Ethical Standards and Integrity, 3.4. Conflicts of interest.
15 Principle 3 – Ethical Standards and Integrity, 3.6. Contract management and tendering.
16 Principle 3 – Ethical Standards and Integrity, 3.8. Fight against doping.
17 Principle 3.9. Fight against manipulation of competitions.
18 Principle 3.10. Safeguarding.

19 Principle 3.11 Reporting mechanisms.
20 Principle 3.12. Education, training and internal communication.
21 Principle 4.1. Financial transparency.
22 Principle 6, Solidarity – Social and sustainable development through sport, Principle 6.1. Distribution of resources.
23 Principle 7 – Autonomy of the Olympic Movement – Harmonious relations with government authorities and external partners; 7.2. Co-operation and co-ordination with government authorities and external partners.
24 Rule 3.5 of the OC.
25 Article 1, Paragraph 4 of the "Rules of Conduct for the Recognised International Federations seeking inclusion in the Olympic Games Organising Committee proposal on additional sports (Implementing Rule of the IOC Code of Ethics)".
26 "Definition of 'Participants' in the Olympic Games – Implementing Rule of the IOC Code of Ethics".
27 Rule 26.1.3.
28 Rule 29.
29 Rule 3.2, *in fine*.
30 Rule 2.1.
31 Rule 27.2.2.1.
32 Rule 27.2.2.2.
33 Rule 27.2.2.5.
34 Rule 27.2.2.6.
35 Rule 27.2.2.7.
36 Rule 27.5.
37 Rule 27.6.
38 Rule 27.7.7.2.
39 Rule 27.9.
40 Bye-law to Rules 27 and 28, no. 1.3.
41 Rule 33.3.
42 Rule 35.3.
43 Bye-law to Rule 40, no. 3.
44 Bye-law to Rule 40, paragraph 3.
45 Article 14, first paragraph of the IOC Code of Ethics.
46 Article 17 of the "Rules of Conduct for Continuous Dialogue with Interested Parties – Future Host Elections (IOC Code of Ethics Implementation Rule)".
47 Article 27 of the "Rules of Conduct for a Targeted Dialogue – Future Elections to Host the Olympic Games (Implementing Rules of the IOC Code of Ethics)". Registration must be finalised before any services are provided and/or any consultancy work is supported by the Preferred City. The registration process as well as the "IOC Rules on the Registration of Consultants" is published in the IOC Code of Ethics. Failure to comply with these rules will lead to the application of sanctions as set out in the "IOC Rules on the Registration of Consultants" – cf. Article 28. Violations of the Rules of Conduct will be dealt with by the IOC Chief Ethics and Compliance Officer. Any serious or repeated violation must be referred to the IOC Ethics Commission – cf. Article 35.

48 Article 1, first paragraph of the "IOC Rules on the Registration of Consultants". The entry in the Register is made by the consultant by means of a written document in which it undertakes to respect the fundamental ethical principles, the CO, the "IOC Code of Ethics and its Implementing Rules", particularly the "Rules of Conduct for a Continuous and Targeted Dialogue with Stakeholders and the Rules on Conflicts of Interest". Article 2, first paragraph of the "IOC Rules on the Registration of Consultants". Any failure to respect the ethical principles of the IOC, the OC, the IOC Code of Ethics and the Implementing Rules, in particular the "Rules of Conduct for a Continuous and Targeted Dialogue with Stakeholders and the Rules on Conflicts of Interest" may lead to a sanction imposed by the IOC Executive Board such as withdrawal of registration for a specific period of time or a reprimand, together with the publication of an official IOC communiqué. In the "Consultant's Declaration of Consent", the Consultant states (and signs) that he/she has taken note of the Olympic Charter, the IOC Code of Ethics, and the respective Implementing Rules, particularly the "Rules of Conduct for a Continuous and Targeted Dialogue with Stakeholders, the Rules on Conflicts of Interest and the IOC Rules for the Registration of Consultants" – Article 4, "Declaration of Consent by the Consultant". The Consultant will also declare to respect these texts and submit any related disputes to the CAS – Article 4 of the "IOC Rules on the Registration of Consultants".

49 Article 8 of the "Rules of Conduct for a Targeted Dialogue – Future Elections to Host the Olympic Games (Implementing Rules of the IOC Code of Ethics)".

50 Article 1 of the "Rules of Conduct for Continuous Dialogue – Future Elections to Host the Olympic Games (Implementing Rules of the IOC Code of Ethics)".

51 Article 2.

52 Rule 40.

53 Rule 43.

54 Bye-law to Rule 44, no. 4.

55 Bye-law to Rule 44, no. 6.

56 Rule 45.3.

57 Rule 45.3.3.

58 Rule 18–3.10.

59 Rules Implementing the Statutes of the IOC Ethics Commission, B. Procedure for analysing and investigating complaints, reports or acts with a view to submitting them to the IOC Ethics Commission, Article 18.

3 The legal nature of the three main constituents of the Olympic Movement

The legal nature of the IOC

For many years, while the "Olympic Law" remained in force, the legal nature of the IOC was never defined,[1] perhaps because the IOC has always been confronted with the contradiction between its legally recognised status as a private law association in and its current conduct as a particular type of public law organisation.

The "Olympic Rules" published in 1908 referred to the IOC as a *permanent* organisation but said nothing about its legal nature. This omission persisted for some years.

In 1920, the Lausanne City Council enquired into the legality of the IOC and the legitimacy of Pierre de Coubertin's signature on the document, which established the headquarters of the IOC in Lausanne, as this had not been ratified in any way by the IOC Session.

A lawyer consulted by the Lausanne City Council opined, on first considering the matter that the IOC could not be regarded as an association in Swiss law, and so could not be considered a corporate person with the capacity to enter into contracts. He accordingly suggested the statutes be reviewed. After a second examination, the lawyer deemed it prudent to require that the IOC be entered in the Lausanne Commercial Registry, with express mention of the persons qualified to act in its name and to represent it.

Pierre de Coubertin reacted negatively, as he wished to prevent the IOC from being treated as a mere association in Swiss law, obliged to register as if it were *any common High Street business*. Pierre de Coubertin aspired to the IOC being placed on an equal footing with international organisations like the (then) League of Nations.[2]

The ambiguity as to the legal nature of the IOC persisted for several decades until the need to clarify the situation finally became unavoidable. In 1974, a commission was appointed with the task of studying this issue in depth, with two guiding principles, one positive – the interest that the IOC and its members and staff might have in the legal personality of the IOC being recognised – and the other negative – without prejudice to the fact that the

DOI: 10.4324/9781003569749-4

legitimacy of the IOC to sue and be sued IOC had up to that point been recognised, it was feared that others might come forward to pursue the IOC in the courts, either to claim rights based on contract or statute or else to denigrate the image of the IOC.

In October 1974, at the 75th Session of the IOC in Vienna, a definition of the legal nature of the IOC was finally approved and embodied in the then Rule 11(2) of the OC, defining the IOC as "*an association in international law with a legal personality, of unlimited duration and with its registered office in Switzerland*". Therefore, the IOC was defined as an entity governed by international law, with its own legal status, and independent of national laws.

This wording created the risk of a misconception that the IOC had international legal personality, which was strengthened given: (i) The Olympic Charter's (OC) authority over states; (ii) The enormous range of contracts concluded between the IOC, specialised UN agencies and even states and (iii) The IOC's capacity to present claims against international organisations.

The rule therefore had to be reviewed to remove the confusion. Accordingly, several years later, in 1991, the (then) Rule 19 of the OC attempted a clearer statement by defining the IOC as "*an international non-governmental non-profit organisation, constituted as an association with legal personality, recognised by a decree of the Swiss Federal Council dated 17 September 1981.*"

In the current version of the OC, Rule 15(1) is practically the same, albeit updated: "*The IOC is an international non-governmental not-for-profit organisation, of unlimited duration, in the form of an association with the status of a legal person, recognised by the Swiss Federal Council in accordance with an agreement entered into on 1 November 2000.*"

It seems to us that the OC has, since 1991, stated the true legal nature of the IOC.

Above all, the IOC is an organisation with an international character – not to be confused with an international organisation, in the legal sense of the term[3] – this can be explained not only by the many nationalities of its members and of the constituents of the OM but also by its international vocation as expressed in terms almost of a public service mission within the international legal order, by way of humanist and ethical missions, established in partnership with, or with the permission and recognition of states, and intergovernmental organisations. Indeed, the Swiss Federal Council itself recognises that the activities undertaken by the IOC have a *worldwide dimension* and emphasises both the *universal role* of the IOC in the context of international relations and its *renown* throughout the world.

Secondly, the IOC is a non-governmental organisation. It could not be defined otherwise, in our view, because, as we have seen, the OC – adopted and modified by an IOC body, the Session – is the constitutive document of the IOC, which is thus not founded on any international or intergovernmental agreement, treaty or convention. Moreover, the logic of the IOC is based squarely on its independence of government intervention and never in its history has it sought consultative status at the UN, although the possibility has been tabled and the IOC fulfils the requirements for such status, precisely because of its wish to remain completely autonomous vis-à-vis international governmental organisations.

Another important feature of the IOC's legal status is the fact that it has legal personality within Swiss law, conferred by the Swiss Federal Constitution, which guarantees freedom of association, and by the Swiss Civil Code, which, respectively, make provision regarding legal personality and associations. As its registered office and place of operation is in Lausanne, Switzerland, it is governed in accordance with the domestic law of the Swiss state and so derives its rights and obligations under that law.

None of the earlier prevents the IOC's legal personality being viewed at the same time in the light of Articles 1 and 2 of the "European Convention on the Recognition of the Legal Personality of International Non-Governmental Organisations", adopted by the Council of Europe, the criteria of which seem to be fully satisfied by the IOC: (i) it has a non-profit-making aim of international utility; (ii) it has been established by an instrument governed by the internal law of a Party – in this case Switzerland; (iii) it carries on its activities with effect in at least two States; (iv) it has its statutory office in the territory of a Party and the central management and control in the territory of that Party or of another Party – in this case Switzerland and (v) the IOC's legal personality and capacity are recognised as of right in the other parties signatory to the Convention.

Firstly, in support of what has been said about the legal status of the IOC, there seems to be no doubt of the fact that the legal recognition of the IOC and the privileges granted to it, having been conferred unilaterally by the Swiss Federal Council, which reinforces the conclusion that the IOC is not a *subject of public international law*.[4]

The legal nature of the National Olympic Committees

The OC attempts to exert a harmonising influence on the ordering of National Olympic Committees (NOCs), but does not lay down uniform requirements as to their legal nature, which would in any case be impracticable given the different types of legislation in force in the various countries that have NOCs.

Accordingly, there are significant differences from country to country.

While some NOCs were created by law (such as the NOC in the USA, created by the *Amateur Sports Act* and the NOC in Jordan, established by the Jordanian Olympic Committee Law No. 13 for the Year 2007), others are not, but are subject to specific rules contained in the State law (as in the case of both the Portuguese and Spanish Olympic Committee), and there is also a category of NOC that is not even mentioned in any law, as in the case of the NOC in Switzerland. A few NOCs were created through an incorporation act

(Australian Olympic Committee Inc.) or a Company Act (For instance, the Barbados Olympic Association Inc. or the Olympic Federation of Ireland). On the other hand, the fact of being a non-profit association does not prevent some NOCs from expressly stating in their Statutes that their mission is (also) to organise and coordinate sponsoring activities; to organise and co-organise advertising campaigns or the marketing of brands via merchandising and remaining commercial activities; to buy and sell promotional material and sport equipment; to do lobbying and to find sponsors (see, in particular, the Belgium Olympic Committee and the Hellenic Olympic Committee in what regards specifically "Concluding sponsorship agreements").

Most NOCs have private legal status and are completely independent of public authorities. However, there are cases where the former does not necessarily imply the latter. For example, the CNOSF in France, although it is an association under private law, it is also invested by the law with a public service mission, and therefore its statutes must by law be approved by the French Council of State decree. Similarly, while it is true that in the US the USOC has wide autonomy and receives little public subsidy, it is nevertheless obliged under the act that created it to provide the House of Representatives, the Senate and the President with a quadrennial report on its activities. On the other hand, the Italian example is unique, having a dual function and a hybrid nature: CONI is a public body and is simultaneously a confederation of national sports federations; it has a fiduciary relationship with the IOC but is also the public body that oversees the entire organisation and regulation of Italian sport. Finally, one might also refer the example of the National Olympic Committee of the Republic of Kazakhstan, defined by a Charter as a "*Public Association*".

The legal nature of the International Sports Federations

International Federations (IFs) are associations of associations, to the extent that they bring together various national federations, with legal personality based on the laws of the country in which they are established. IFs are all Non-Governmental Organisations.

Notes

1 According to M. BERLIOUX, "[o]*nly from the 60s was the IOC seen as an association governed by Swiss law. Until then it was, legally speaking, a sort of ectoplasm, but it was content to be so, since it could thus do whatever it wanted without submitting to the diktat of an international or national jurisdiction*", *Revue Juridique et Ecónomique du Sport*, September 2002, page 31.

2 V.C. GILLIÉRON, Les relations de Lausanne et du Mouvement Olympique à l'époque de Pierre de Coubertin 1894–1939, Lausanne – IOC, 1993, pages 92–93.

3 The IOC does not fulfil the three necessary and sufficient conditions to be considered as an international organisation, namely (i) consisting of States, (ii) being constituted by a Convention and (iii) having legal autonomy *vis-à-vis* its members.

4 On this point, see Fernando Xarepe Silveiro, "O Empréstimo Internacional de Futebolistas Profissionais", *Estudos de Direito Desportivo*, Coimbra, Almedina, 2002, page 121.

Part II

Olympism, Olympic Games and human rights

4 Sport, human rights and the legacy of Pierre de Coubertin[1]

Introduction

Coubertin was born, in Paris, on 1 January 1863, into an aristocratic family, and died, in Geneva, on 2 September 1937, aged 74, destitute and ignored, particularly by his compatriots. He died before the adoption of the major international Human Rights texts, but was born 74 years after the approval of the "Declaration of the Rights of Man and of the Citizen" by French National Constituent Assembly on 26 August 1789. The fact that he had been both wealthy and with reduced means enabled him to understand the importance of equality between human beings whatever their social status.

It is essential, in order to understand this relationship, to consider de Coubertin's profile as a jurist and the influence of his academic and legal background on his concept of the Ethics of Sport, in general, and of the Ethics of Olympism, in particular. This is because de Coubertin's law-based ethical approach is one of the legacies he left us, which enables us to regard sport as a human right, as stated in the Olympic Charter, but which international legal instruments between states still disregard. These matters are comprised in the first and the second parts of this chapter.

The third part of this chapter focuses on sport as an autonomous human right, based on the contribution of Pierre de Coubertin, and goes on to consider another aspect, also on the basis of the French Baron's ideas and work, that is, sport as an instrument for the promotion of human rights.

Coubertin: from reluctant jurist to the precursor of law-based "Olympic Ethics"

The relationship between Pierre de Coubertin and law starts with the fact that the Baron was a law graduate. However, this academic *background* was in no way the realisation of any of his various ambitions.

According to Louis Callebat,[2] Pierre de Coubertin's matriculation at the Faculty of Law was solely a matter of family tradition, and it was this that led Coubertin to study law, out of respect for his father, Baron Charles Fredy,

DOI: 10.4324/9781003569749-6

who was a respected jurist and a judge. The study of law was therefore not Coubertin's choice, vocation or an ambition with a view to a successful future professional career.

However, Coubertin was also the indirect author of this decision, because his parents insisted that he study law, when he refused to follow a career in the army, that is, when Coubertin was confronted with the typical career options of young men of his social class, that is, the army or the law, Coubertin resolved the dilemma by choosing the law. However, this option proved burdensome, for, as Coubertin confessed in his Memoirs: "I *hated my law studies. Not only because they were boring but also because they were humiliating. I did not attend a single class. I went to the faculty to matriculate. It was a torment to have to wear the black gown with a white hood that examinees were required to wear on the day of the annual examination. Only God knows how I suffered!"*

Coubertin's rejection of the law naturally did not affect his lucidity and sang-froid and caused him to reject the role of law in his Olympic project. It would not be feasible for a sport and social project of such magnitude to be created without the assistance of law and its inherent coactivity.

Nevertheless, Coubertin always resisted the abundance of rules. Primarily, in order to defend the autonomy of sports organisations, which is still frequently asserted, about which Coubertin stated, "*The more regulations they adopt, the more constrained they become. Give Olympic organisations some flexibility."*[3] Likewise, and perhaps with the benefit of his albeit reluctant legal training, Coubertin advised the various countries regarding the risks that could be incurred via the adoption of complicated legislation, which is full of commitments and contradictions. Coubertin's profile was undoubtedly that of a leader, who introduced as few rules as possible. For example, it was only in 1908 (12 years after the emergence of the Olympic Games of the Modern Era) that the International Olympic Committee was created, which worked for 14 years with very few regulations that governed either its internal organisation or, more importantly, the holding of the Olympic Games.

In the recent 2020 Tokyo Olympic Games, which were postponed to 2021 because of the pandemic, the oath made by players, athletes, trainers and referees, was altered, in accordance with a recommendation made by the Olympic Athletes Commission, to include the words "*inclusion"* and "*equality*", so as to read as follows: "*We promise to take part in these Olympic Games, respecting and abiding by the rules and in the spirit of fair play, inclusion and equality. Together we stand in solidarity and commit ourselves to sport without doping, without cheating, without any form of discrimination. We do this for the honour of our teams, in respect for the Fundamental Principles of Olympism, and to make the world a better place through sport*." Anyone, who heard this oath during the opening ceremony of the most important sports event in the world, or who has just learnt about it by reading this, will say that it is difficult not to be cynical about such declarations, and to regard anyone, who believes in the purity of sport, in general, and in the Olympic ideals, in particular, as ingenuous, given the frequent negative news stories about sport. However, the reason for such an oath can easily be understood, that is, it is necessary to strive for ethical and non-discriminatory sport.

These efforts are not a recent phenomenon. The need for such efforts was already recognised by Pierre de Coubertin, who, in 1920, introduced an Olympic oath in the following terms, at the Olympic Games of the Modern Era: "I *promise, in the name of all competitors, that we will participate in these Olympic Games, while respecting and obeying the rules to which we are subject, in the true sporting spirit, for the glory of sport and the honour of our teams."*

In 1920, there was none of the commercialisation, professionalisation or globalisation of sport that exists today, which gives a lie to the idea that fraud and inequality in sport are a consequence of the fact that sport has moved away from amateurism and minimal massification. This conclusion leads us to ask why the self-same Coubertin, who exalted these principles, rules and values as inherent in sport, considered that the athletes' oath was of fundamental importance. The truth is that the oath was one of the aspects that Coubertin took from the Olympic Games of Antiquity, and revived. He certainly did this because he understood the timelessness of the need to commit to the rules.

In 776 BCE, athletes, coaches, judges, relatives, friends, aliptas (slaves who anointed the athletes) and alitas (guards) had to take a solemn oath before an imposing statue of Zeus, "Sovereign of Olympus", the "Oath-God", and over the palpitating strips of boar flesh that were offered to him.

The oath was sport-related, and also connected to ethical and deontological issues, as a tool of preventive adhesion or incorporation to the rules. The pain for the oath violation was perjury. The function of oaths in sport and in other areas (e.g. in medicine, in the case of the famous Hippocratic oath) was to consolidate and strengthen contracts. Oaths were a more intensive and effective form of self-commitment, in the presence of witnesses, a guarantee, and a subjection to divine authority, in the event of breach.

We can now understand that the awareness that sport can involve unethical conduct dates back to the earliest days of sport competition in Ancient Greece, and that conduct that sought to vitiate competition results existed in those days, so that the oath was a preventive measure employed to combat such undesirable conduct. The matter essentially at issue was corruption, as violence was uncommon, and doping did not yet exist. Filostratus explained this phenomenon as a loosening of customs and a pleasure-seeking attitude that arose among athletes, because of their corrupt lust for money, and the consequent practice of buying and selling victories. The situation was also vitiated by the conduct of coaches and representatives, who had little concern for their own ethics, or the ethics of athletes, and whose major concern was their own gain. There is also another possible explanation, that is, some athletes, who were accustomed to a luxurious life, preferred to lose the Games voluntarily, in exchange for a good bribe. There is also another possible reason: corruption did not result in the forfeiture of the winner's title and crown, even though it involves a heavy penalty. Furthermore, we cannot overlook another aspect that could explain this corruption, that is, the rivalry between cities, and political disputes, as the crowning ceremonies involved the exaltation of the athlete, his father, and the city/community to which they belonged. An even more simple explanation, given by the Greek philosopher Lucianus, also cannot be excluded, that is, that corruption could simply be a consequence of an athlete's dishonesty, of the desire to win at any price or of despair that caused the athlete to cheat. This explains why, notwithstanding the oath, there were various cases of corruption in the Olympic Games of Antiquity, all of which resulted in the imposition of penalties by the Olympic Senate, which were duly publicised, for the purposes of transparency, deterrence and prevention.

Coubertin, who based himself on history, which he valued much more than law, understood the need to retain and preserve the oath, for the reasons stated, and in terms very similar to the original, particularly in the context of modern sport that will always attract more corruption. For, while corruption has apparently been inherent in sports competitions since the earliest days, there was then only one winner, and no records, unlike the Olympic Games that Coubertin revived.

Coubertin's motives can therefore easily be inferred. Namely, that the prior assumption, by the sportspersons involved in the Olympic Games, of an obligation to comply with the rules, would ensure compliance with Sport Ethics and Olympic Ethics prior to the Olympic Games.

The "Ethical asset inherent in the nature of sport as a human right": Pierre de Coubertin and "sport for all"

Human rights: the concept and legal protection of it in international law

The United Nations (UN) defines human rights as "*universal legal rights that protect individuals and groups from the acts or omissions of governments that infringe human dignity*".[4] Human rights are therefore a series of rules that are intended to defend the human person against abuses of power by the state bodies. "The basis of the concept of human rights is the concept of the inherent human dignity of all members of the human family." The principle of human dignity is essentially a general and reciprocal duty, of each person in relation to all other persons, and a duty to respect their dignity.

Human rights are universal, inalienable (no one, other than the existing legal order, may deprive anyone of the said rights), indivisible or inseparable, interdependent or complementary, irrevocable (cannot be abolished), non-transferrable to third parties, and cannot be renounced or waived.

Human rights are crafted by the constituent legislators as fundamental rights, and are defined as such in the international human rights instruments. Human rights are overarching in relation to the internal constitutional legal order, as autonomous personal rights, which are guaranteed by international law.

Human rights can be placed in different categories, that is, human rights that are intended to ensure freedom, which are referred to as first-generation human rights, rights that seek to establish equality, which are called second-generation human rights, and third-generation human rights, which enshrine the aspiration of fraternity and solidarity. When considered in greater detail, civil and political rights are first-generation rights, that is, the right to life, the prohibition of torture, degrading treatment and slavery; and the non-retroactivity of criminal law; economic, social and cultural rights are second-generation rights, for example, the right to education, the right to participate in cultural life and the right to benefit from scientific progress; the new rights, or third-generation rights, include the right to a healthy environment; the right to development; the right to peace and security and the right to the common heritage of mankind. However, there are schools of thought that identify fourth-generation rights, that is, rights that claim new social models. These rights include technology society rights and also, for example, matters related to biology/genetics.

There are various international protection systems in the international human rights framework, which are as follows: the worldwide system, on the one hand, and regional systems, on the other, that is, the European system, the European Union system, the US system and the African system. There are various regional organisations that issue human rights rules, such as the United Nations (UN) and its specialised agencies, the Council of Europe, and the Organisation of African Unity, which is now called the African Union.

Given the international nature of these organisations, there are many multilateral treaties that protect human rights, which include general and more sectoral treaties. These multiple sources combine in the various systems referred to earlier, that is, in the universal system, within the UN, of which the primary instrument is the 1948 Universal Declaration of Human Rights (UDHR), although it is not legally binding. The international regional protection of human rights essentially involves the following:

a) In the European system, of the Council of Europe, the Convention for the Protection of Human Rights and Fundamental Freedoms, the 1950 European Human Rights Convention (EHRC), which is particularly important, alongside other important sources, particularly the 1966 International Covenant on Civil and Political Rights (ICCPR), and the 1966 International Covenant on Economic, Social and Cultural Rights (ICESCR), which give binding legal effect to human rights and guarantee many substantive rights.

b) The relevant instrument in the European Union system is the 2000 Charter of Fundamental Freedoms.
c) In the American system, within the ambit of the Organisation of American States, the relevant instrument is the 1948 American Declaration of Human Rights and Duties.
d) In the African system, within the ambit of the African Union, the primary instrument is the African Charter on Human and People's Rights, which was issued by the Organisation of African Unity, which is now the African Union, in 1981.

The right to sport as a human right

Further to the Fourth Fundamental Principle of the Olympic Charter, "[t]he *of sport is a human right. Every individual must have the possibility of practising sport, without discrimination of any kind and in the Olympic spirit, which requires mutual understanding with a spirit of friendship, solidarity and fair play" (Olympic Charter, Fourth Fundamental Principle of Olympism)*. According to natural law theorists, sport is inherent in human beings, because of its essential nature: human access to sport cannot therefore be subject to the whim of legislators, or the opinion of the majority. The Right to Sport always exists, and human beings, because of the essential nature of this right, are always entitled to it. The inclusion of the Right to Sport in international and other legal instruments is therefore merely declarative. Accordingly, and according to this position, sport must be considered to be a human right.

Likewise, if we follow the legal theorist Pierre de Collomb,[5] who maintains that sport is a human activity in the fullest sense of that term, because it is in sport that humans engage their most precious asset, that is, their bodies, we will probably reach the same conclusion that sport should be considered to be a human right.

An identical conclusion can be reached on the basis of the statement in the Introduction of the *World Player Rights Policy*, adopted by the World Players Association: "*Players are first people and then players . . . . Consequently, players are at the intersection between sport and human rights.*" This view of players is supported by the French legal theorist Jean-Pierre MARGUÉNAUD[6] according to whom sport organisations cannot, on the basis of the *Lex Sportiva*, surrender to the temptation to operate in a closed circuit, and evade the influence of human rights, as if sportspersons were somehow not primarily people.

It follows therefore that if sport is deemed to be inherent in the human person, and, as we have seen, there are various ways to reach that conclusion, the Right to Sport can be seen to be based on the fact that sportspersons are human beings, who have the right to practise the sport of their choice,[7] and who are also entitled to invoke human rights in their defence.

However, it should not be thought that this position is generally accepted. If we refer to those constitutions that refer to sport, it will be seen that many of them do not consider sport to be a fundamental right. Furthermore, there are many countries whose constitutions do not even refer to sport.

Moreover, some important court decisions have rejected the view that the Right to Sport is a Fundamental Right/Human Right.

Firstly, the French Conseil d' Etat has already decided (Ordonnance du CE, 22 Octobre 2001, no. 239194, D. 2002, p. 2709) that neither the right to practise sport nor the right to participate in sports competitions is fundamental freedom, as understood by the law (Article 521(2) of the Code of Administrative Justice), notwithstanding the fact that they are a matter of general interest recognised by law, particularly in the case of high-performance sport.

It has also been decided in the United States of America[8] that there is no right to compete in organised sport competitions. This occurred in a country, where Congress refused to legislate a right of athletes to compete internationally, but rather chose to refer to an "*opportunity*" to participate (*Idem*, p. 324), when it was called on to counterpose the right of athletes to choose the sport in which they want to compete, on the one hand, and "*organisational rights*" that decide the eligibility of an athlete (or of a team to which the athlete belongs), to compete in a competition,[9] on the basis of factors such as age, weight, status (i.e. amateur or professional) or the athlete's performance, on the other hand. The World Anti-Doping Code is a relevant source regarding these eligibility criteria and refers to the issue of whether the athlete is, or is not, suspended from participation in an event because of infringement of anti-doping rules, when the "*fundamental right of sportspersons to participate in sports competitions*" is restricted (World Anti-Doping Code, "*Purpose, Scope and Organization of the World Anti-Doping Program and the Code*").

The issue of the relevance of eligibility rules in this debate is also clear in a CAS decision during the Sydney Olympic Games (Arbitration CAS Ad Hoc Division (O.G. Sydney) 00/001 United States Olympic Committee (USOC) and USA Canoe/Kayak/International Olympic Committee (IOC) Award of 13 September 2000, § 26). According to CAS, "*there is no rule of 'fairness', to be derived from the Olympic Charter's acknowledgment that the practice of sport is a fundamental human right, which should under such circumstances create an outer time limit of Olympic ineligibility.*"

Two additional matters are noteworthy regarding the Olympic Charter.

Firstly, the text of Rule 44.3 of the Olympic Charter: "*Any entry is subject to acceptance by the IOC, which may at its discretion, at any time, refuse any entry, without indication of grounds. Nobody is entitled as of right to participate in the Olympic Games.*" A word to the wise.

Secondly, a relevant decision of the IOC Ethics Committee regarding a previous decision of the Management Committee of the FIVB (International Volleyball Federation) regarding the suspension of the Argentinian Volleyball Federation and the resulting suspension of its players from all regional, or world, competitions, that is, the temporary suspension of the exercise of their Right to Sport, entirely for administrative reasons and when the said players were not guilty of any offence in relation to the FIVB. The Ethics Committee's decision contains the following passage: "*The Ethics Committee draws attention to the fact that the right to sport is a fundamental principle and that this right, as recognised and stated in the Olympic Charter, should not be confused with idea of 'sport for all', but extends to all levels of sport, including so-called high-level or international-level sport . . . the Fundamental Principles in the Olympic Charter do not give rise to an unconditional right to participate in competitions; consequently, each International Federation may determine the limits of the said right to participate in competitions, subject to the proviso that the said limits must not be contrary to the Fundamental Principles*" (CAS no. 3/03,*ODEPA/PASO c. FIVB*, award of 21 October 2013). Here too there can be no doubt: there is no right to participate in Olympic Games, and this example can be transposed, *mutatis mutandis*, to other sport events. Accordingly, this right is limited by the eligibility rules regarding participation in events.

Accordingly, while it is clear that the eligibility rules are inapplicable in a non-competitive context, which would certainly open up the possibility that the right to ludic, recreational and informal sport is a human right, it is nevertheless true from the matters just described that it is not clear, or generally accepted, that sport is a human right, *per se*.

It may well be, given the matters described earlier, that one of the reasons that help to explain this situation is the fact, referred to in detail below, that sport is never expressly codified in International Public Law instruments as a human right. For,

> There are no Public International Law instruments in which sport is expressly codified as a human right. A "Universal Declaration of Human Rights" (1948) (UDHR), which is the foundation of the international human rights defense system, refers to conc*epts such as* "well-being" (Article 29(2) and the *right of "every person" "to leisure a*ctivities" (article 24), but does not refer to sport. Prior to the UDHR, the "Complement to the Decl*aration of the Rights of Man" (1936), which was produced by the League of the Rights of Man and Citizen, refers to "time for leisure activities" in the* context of the "right to life" (article 4), but without any express reference to sport. The 'International Pact on Economic, Social and Cultural Rights' (1966) and the 'African Charter on Human and Peoples Rights' (1981) (articles 12(1) and 16) likewise only refer to a right to sport implicitly, when they prescribe that "*Every individual shall have the right to enjoy the best attainable state of physical and mental health*". Even in more recent texts, e.g. the 'European Union Charter of Fundamental Rights' (2000), in which sport might be expected to be a priority, sport is not mentioned.

Curiously, specific intergovernmental instruments such as the "Geneva Convention Relative to the Treatment of Prisoners of War" (1949) enshrine the right to sport in the following terms: "the *Detaining Power shall encourage . . . sports and games amongst prisoners"* and *"shall take the measures necessary to ensure the exercise thereof"* and provides that *"Prisoners shall have opportunities for taking physical exercise, including sports and games."*

Similarly, a Resolution of the UN Economic and Social Committee (1977) provides that *"Every prisoner who is not employed in outdoor work shall have at least one hour of suitable exercise in the open air daily if the weather permits"* (Rule 21 (1)).

There are also three other important UN human rights conventions, that is, the "Convention on the Elimination of All Forms of Discrimination against Women" (1979), according to which equality between men and women presupposes *"The same opportunities to participate actively in sports and physical education*" (Article 10(g)); the "Convention on the Rights of the Child" (1989) which provides the right of the *child "to rest and leisure, to engage in play and recreational activities appropriate to the age of the chi*ld"; and the "Convention on the Rights of Persons with Disabilities" (2006) which provides measures to be implemented by states in order *to permit persons with disabilities to participate in recreation, leisure and sport on an equal basis* (Article 30).

It is understandable, from a historical perspective, that sport was not seen as a priority, so that the right to sport was not viewed as an autonomous right, but rather as an ancillary right, or as a part, or consequence, of other rights. In other words, sport does appear in the main binding International Public Law instruments as a personal right, but is referred to either tacitly, or expressly, as a means to exercise other human rights, or as a means to affirm and protect other human rights.

Soft *law* intergovernmental instruments that refer to sport also have a relevant role, for example, the "UNESCO International Charter of Physical Education and Sport". Article 1 of the 1978 version of the Charter, which is titled *"The practice of physical education and sport is a fundamental right for all"* provides in Article 1.1 that *"Every human being has a fundamental right of access to physical education and sport, which are essential for the full development of his personality."* The 2015 version of the Charter adds *"physical activity"* to the material scope of the right, which is expressly stated to be *"a fundamental right of access"*, and makes increased stress on the principle of equality, as expressed in non-discrimination. The "European Sports Charter" (1992), which was issued under the auspices of the Council of Europe, requires states "*to enable every individual to participate in sport*". This approach converges with the one originated by the "European Sport for All Charter" (1975), according to which *"Every individual shall have the right to participate in sport*" (Article 1).

It is therefore notable that there is no express enshrinement of sport as a human right, at state level. As noted earlier, such a provision can only be found in the Olympic Charter, a document issued by the International Olympic Committee (IOC), a non-governmental body. The Olympic Charter, in the felicitous text adopted in July 1996, defines sport as a human right, in the following terms: *"The practice of sport is a hum*an right. Every individual must have the possibility of practising sport, without discrimination of any kind and in the Olympic spirit, which requires mutual understanding with a spirit of friendship, solidarity and fair play" (Fourth Fundamental Principle of Olympism). Secondly, the *"Defence of and respect for human rights"* is one of the operational requirements that must be implemented by the Organising Committee of the Olympic Games, cf. *"Host City Contracts Operational Requirements"* (June 2018).

The right to sport as a human right: the legacy of Pierre de Coubertin

It must be concluded, in the light of the matters stated earlier, that legislators seem to be unaware of what the Spanish legal theorist Rafael DE ASIS[10] notes in excellent terms: "*In any event, the consideration of sport as a human right means that it must be considered to be an ethical asset and have a basis in law. Accordingly, if sport is to be considered a human right, it has to be presented as a justified moral pretention and be linked to a legal provision. . . . traditionally it has been considered to be an ethically relevant activity (dignified human life, free development of the personality, an instrument that satisfies fundamental legal assets . . .).*"

As we stated earlier, Pierre de Coubertin saw a perfect and necessary symbiosis in the link between law and the Olympic Ethic. This provided a very solid basis for the claim that sport should be enshrined as a human right in international state legal instruments, just as it is enshrined in the Olympic Charter.

Coubertin had a view of Sport and Olympism that was marked by egalitarianism and universalism.

As far as egalitarianism is concerned, Coubertin's thought was in line with what is now referred to as "Sport for All", that is, the idea that everyone, without exception and without unjustified discrimination of any type, is entitled to practise sport: "*Sport is not a luxury object, or an activity for the lazy, or even a muscular compensation of brain work. Sport is a possible and non-work-related source of internal perfection, for everyone. Sport belongs to everyone equally and nothing can replace it when it is lacking. The same can also be said from an ethnic point of view: sport belongs to all races."*

For, as Patrice CHOLLEY[11] stresses, egalitarianism is one of the fundamental ideas in the educational and social thought of Coubertin, and is also the basis of the principle of the systematisation of sport and the promotion of sport at all levels. Regarding this, the said author cites a relevant thought of Coubertin, which, we think, demonstrates that sport places the aristocrat and the plebeian on the same level, to a certain extent: *"The advance of sport irritates the defenders of class war and is sympathised with by those who seek more peaceful ways to achieve the changes they desire in the way society is organised. The practice of physical exercise does not create more equal social conditions, but does make social relations more equal, and it is probable that, in this, shape is more important than background."*

Fortunately, this approach of Coubertin continues today and appears in the foundational texts of sports organisations, such as the Olympic Charter, issued by the IOC, and the FIFA Statutes (see, for example, Article 4 of the FIFA Statutes), which enshrine a proclamation of non-discrimination. Sport organisations essentially converge in the proclamation of the texts of International Public Law, which prohibit all discrimination on the grounds of sex, race, colour, nationality, language, religion or opinions, public or other opinion, national, ethnic or social origin, membership of a national majority, fortune/wealth, birth, property, disability, age, or sexual orientation.

However, it is obviously necessary, in the interest of intellectual rigour and honesty, also to mention the misogynist views of Coubertin, who forbade women to participate in the Olympic Games. We do not sympathise with this opinion, but with the opposite view, according to which *"the roots of the participation of women in sport lie deep in human rights."*[12] Nevertheless, and not wishing to excuse or launder Coubertin's position, it is no misinterpretation of his ideas to state that, other than a very personal view of the role of women in society, and the vulnerability and fragility of their bodies, when compared to men, Coubertin makes a distinction between the issue of access to sport, regarding which he did not have a markedly discriminatory view of the status of men and women, *and access* to competitive sport, particularly the Olympic Games, in which he considered women not to be fit to participate. In other words, and in line with what we stated earlier regarding position in legal theory and case law that there is no right to participate in the Olympic Games, Coubertin considered that the sex/gender-based eligibility requirements for a mega-event such as the Olympic Games were justified.

Coubertin had a very clear view regarding universalism: "*The fundamental rule of modern Olympics is based on two words: All Games, All Nations, and not even International Olympic Committee, the highest authority regarding such matters, has the power to change this. I add that a nation is not necessarily an independent state, and that the geography of sport may sometimes differ from political geography.*"[13] The slogan "*All Games, All Nations*" was introduced in 1912, and was intended to signify Coubertin's intent to create a "community" of all sports, and athletes from all nations, a type of Janus, with his two faces, that is, the national face and the international face. Coubertin's thought did not appear to contain any aim to mitigate national pride and belonging, by subsuming them in a larger and internationalist project. His aim was to achieve coexistence between internationalism and patriotism, through sport, in a context in which respect and non-discrimination would vanquish oppression, and defeat violence and destruction, and therefore contribute to international reconciliation between peoples, with a view to peace.

The meaning and scope of Internationalism and Universalism are so convergent that the following passage from the "Sport Reform Charter", dated 13 September 1930, combines and summarises them in a manner that clarifies the thought of Coubertin: "N*o nation, no class, and no occupations are excluded.*"

The role of sport in the promotion of other human rights: the legacy of Pierre de Coubertin

> "Olympism is a philosophy of life, exalting and combining in a balanced whole the qualities of body, will and mind. Blending sport with culture and education, Olympism seeks to create a way of life based on the joy of effort, the educational value of good example, social responsibility and respect for universal fundamental ethical principles."
>
> *"The goal of Olympism is to place sport at the service of the harmonious development of humankind, with a view to promoting a peaceful society concerned with the preservation of human dignity."*
>
> *(First and Second Fundamental Principles of Olympism)*

The role of sport in the promotion of other human rights

In addition to the aspect of sport as an autonomous Human Right, there is another facet to the relationship between Sport and Human Rights, which we shall now consider: Sport as a factor ancillary to other human rights, on the basis that it is possible to attain other human rights via sport,[14] and that sport must be used as a vehicle to promote other human rights. In fact, sport may even be a tool to promote respect for the fundamental values in the UDHR.[15] Here too, Pierre de Coubertin also left a tangible legacy, which we shall now explain briefly.

Education via sport

It can be said that Pierre de Coubertin's project was more an educational project than a sport project, or at least that the project was equally an educational project and a sport project, in various respects.

Coubertin viewed sport primarily as an educational resource: the issue was not the education of the body, or by the body, but the education of the human being, as a whole, with a stress on the building of character through sport, so that the Olympic Games was a symbol, and an example to fortify the objectives of sport.

Coubertin thought that an educated person would be more aware of his/her value, but would also be aware of the limits of their knowledge, which is something that is inextricably linked to international relations and the search for peace[16]: for Coubertin education through sport (an athletic education) was a first step towards education for peace, that is, in the context of a reform of the university education system: "*demand higher education in all countries as a basis for peace between peoples*".[17]

According to Coubertin, sport and physical education were also a successful tool to put an end to aggression, which the Baron considered to be intrinsic and spontaneous in human beings. Accordingly, the virile energy of sport would help to shape the character of human beings in their daily relationship with themselves, and their neighbours. The educational reform that Coubertin sought to implement was therefore based on a type of physical education unlike that then prevalent, which focused on gymnastics based on analytic, rigid and authoritarian exercises which were primarily intended to train male pupils. Until then, physical education was essentially intended to strengthen the body and the character, in a manner very similar to military training, as a way to control the agonistic and competitive tendencies typical of adolescence and youth, particularly among boys (via a focus on the "races" as a basis of a masculine sense of duty) with a need for self-affirmation, which was a quality that Coubertin wished to discourage.

Coubertin was primarily opposed to German militarised athletics and to Swedish gymnastics, both of which were marked by an authoritarianism, which disregarded experimental pedagogy. Coubertin's insistence on gymnastics reveals his view that sport based on hierarchy and obedience, which led to uniformity of conduct and blind discipline, was dangerous and would contribute to the promotion of nationalism and militarism, opposed by Coubertin's pacifism.[18]

What Coubertin wanted was sport based on social, moral and patriotic virtues, with a liberating, solidary and unifying ethos, which was able to both pacify and virilise young people. This idea was to be implemented via the introduction of sports and games in secondary schools, as a part of physical education classes. In his anxiousness for peace, Coubertin insisted on showing that a child's school years were a stage of life in which experience of freedom should be permitted, and physical vigour should be promoted, without repressing bodily impulses. Secondary education was therefore a stage in which children and young people should be educated and guided, but not for political and religious manipulation. The view of education as an "initial phase of life", a source of human progress, and an ethical challenge was central to the Olympic Movement.

This entire view of Coubertin amounted to an understanding that sport is an essential component of the development of the personality of all citizens, and is a vehicle of formal and informal education. The body and the mind are educated through sport. Sport is therefore one among other aspects of the human right to education, as provided in Article 26 of the UDHR. Which states, in paragraph 1, that "everyone has the right to education", and in paragraph 2 that "*Education shall be directed to the full development of the human personality and to the strengthening of respect for human rights and fundamental freedoms. It shall promote understanding, tolerance, and friendship among all nations, racial or religious groups, and shall further the activities of the United Nations for the maintenance of peace*." For the reasons already stated, which will be discussed further in section 3.1.5, this paragraph 2 could easily have been written by Pierre de Coubertin, as is evident from the keywords it contains, that is, "human personality"; "understanding"; "all nations"; "all racial groups" and "peace".

It is particularly noteworthy in this regard that the UN has argued for the inclusion of adequate physical education provision in the curriculums of children and young people, which includes the presence of qualified personnel, and is not considered to be either play or entertainment.[19] The UN has argued that education systems should provide information regarding the impact of the acquisition of healthy lifestyles, which also provides children and young people with the information they need in order to make informed decisions.[20]

Sport as a promoter of the right to health

Coubertin stressed that "*good health is a prerequisite for a full life, as we lose time when we are ill, and time is money.*"[21] As we have seen, Coubertin's entire educational project was focused on the harmonious physical and mental health of young athletes. Sport as a promoter of health really was one of Coubertin's objectives. However, the Baron went even further in the link between Sport and Health, and, in the final chapter of his famous Olympic Memoirs, which were published in 1930, argued "*against excessive training*", a phenomenon which still exists, while also, and in a very contemporary approach, defending the "*development of a sport medicine based on the state of health rather than the morbid case, which is very sharply focused on the examination of the individual's psychological characteristics*". It can therefore also be said that Coubertin viewed the link between Sport and Health, both in terms of sport as a means to promote health and prevent illness and in terms of the protection of the health of sportspersons.

Sport and Health are closely linked.

According to the Preamble of the Constitution of the World Health Organisation, "*Health is a state of complete physical, mental, and social well-being and not merely the absence of disease or infirmity. The enjoyment of the highest attainable standard of health is one of the fundamental rights of every human being without distinction of race, religion, political belief, economic or social condition. The health of all peoples is fundamental to the attainment of peace and security and is dependent upon the fullest co-operation of individuals and States.*"

The right of citizens to health is a prerequisite of a dignified life and involves the positive obligation of states to take measures to combat and prevent health hazards, to promote healthy lifestyles and to improve the general well-being of the public, which necessarily includes the promotion of physical activity, physical exercise and lifelong sport. Citing Ângelo VARGAS and Eliane CUNHA GONÇALVES,[22] *"as far as the specific issue of health is concerned, it should be noted that the social sciences have long since identified the epistemological characteristics that enable us to understand that basic attention to the health of the public involves nutritional education, the practice of physical exercise and sport, as preventive measures, with a view to good levels of health. In this, leisure and sport activities are an essential aspect of education, culture, and health."*

Measures that promote health for all, that is, public health, must therefore include measures to promote sport for all, in order to achieve health through sport. There can be no doubt that sport is one of the ways to recognise "*the right of all people to enjoy the best possible state of physical and mental health*" (Article 12 OHCHR) and with this, "*well-being*" (Article 25 UDHN). Sport therefore promotes health, as a way to promote "*the right of all people to enjoy the best possible state of physical and* mental health", as provided in Article 12(1) of the ICESCR.

Sport and the right to culture

When Pierre de Coubertin created the Olympic Games of the Modern Era, one of his aims was to provide athletes, particularly young athletes, with regular opportunities to meet in stadiums and together to become aware of the existence of an infinite and diversified world that exists beyond living environment. The Olympic Games were conceived as intercultural meetings that contribute to peace, via a mutual understanding of historical cultures (sharing of knowledge regarding the historical heritage of different countries).

According to Coubertin, physical education and sport education is a unique and incessant carrier of cultural education and cultural dissemination, that is, sport is a cultural tool. It is therefore unsurprising that the French Baron included artistic and musical contests in the Olympic Games, alongside sport competitions.

Given the universal character of the Games, Coubertin managed to democratise sport and culture, while also stressing the inextricable link between them. Accordingly, when we read Article 15(1)(c) of the ICESCR, which enshrines the "*Right of all to participate in cultural activity*", we understand that events such as the Olympic Games embody this right. Practising and watching various sports with differing origins, backgrounds and roots, which involve people from more than 200 countries, is clearly a moment of cultural enjoyment.

Sport and the right to a fair and equitable trial

In 1909, in a speech that Coubertin made regarding amateurism, he invoked the need for "*a single and absolutely independent court*" that provided "*guarantees*", "*a sort of Hague Court for sport*".[23]

Coubertin's concerns regarding the independence of what is now referred to as "*sports justice*" had already been expressed publicly, in 1907, in another speech, which concerned the "role of the federations", which included the following remarks: "*The first and most vital of tasks which falls to a sports federation is to organize itself judicially. Indeed, it must be once a council of state, a court of appeal and a jurisdiction court. Its job is to maintain rules, interpret them and give judgement at last instance; it has to ratify or overturn expulsions; it has to intervene between clubs and impose solutions to collective disputes. Now if there is one quality which a judicial apparatus must possess, it is of course independence. Independence in this case is achieved by the constitution within the federation of a judicial board whose members must not include anyone who is an active member of any of the groups whose interests are at issue. It will be composed of former sportsmen, and mature men of sufficient experience. The federation can either leave it up to them to recruit their membership, or undertake this itself, on condition that it appoints them for a specific term of office, at least three to five years. An organization resembling this who thinks about this will clearly see the vital need to adopt it, if one is concerned about rendering the most elementary form of justice. How can one accept having the delegates of clubs as both judge and party, being called upon to assess the fairness of measures directly involving their colleagues and clubs?*"[24]

Coubertin wanted an international court for sport, which provided the necessary guarantees. Decades later, another President of the IOC, Juan Antonio Samaranch, triggered the creation of the Court of Arbitration for Sport, in Lausanne (TAS/CAS).

Although he did not use terms such as "autonomy of sport" and "specificity of sport" that are currently in vogue, Coubertin also advocated self-regulation, because he supported the operation of sports justice under the auspices of the sports federations. Coubertin also supported recourse to specialist judges and the existence and application of rules regarding conflicts of interest. This demonstrates his fundamental concern that decisions should be independent.

The independence/impartiality of CAS has been considered by the Swiss Federal Court in the *Gundel* decision (TF 4P.217/1992, 15.03.1993) and was recently even the subject of a decision of the European Court of Human Rights, in the famous *Mutu/Pechstein* case (*Mutu and Pechstein v. Switzerland* – 40575/10 and 67474/10, Judgement of 2 October 2018 [Section III]). The issue before the court involved consideration of a CAS arbitration clause provided in the regulations of an international sports federation, that is, the ISU. In its judgement, the European Court of Human Rights considered that notwithstanding the fact that the clause was imposed by the ISU regulations, rather than by law, it was correct to consider that acceptance of the jurisdiction of CAS by the applicant meant that proceedings amounted to compulsory arbitration as understood in the case law of the court. However, CAS considered that there was valid justification for this: namely the interest in allowing conflicts in professional sport, particularly those with an international dimension, to be decided by a specialist and uniform jurisdiction, such as CAS, which operates as a single international court that resolves disputes that are directly, or indirectly, related to sport, quickly and economically. CAS argued further that the Swiss Federal Court has the power to overrule CAS judgements, where basic procedural guarantees are violated, which ensures compliance with Article 6 of the EHRC [this provision provides that *"In the determination of his civil rights and obligations or of any criminal charge against him, everyone is entitled to a fair and public hearing within a reasonable time by an independent and impartial tribunal established by law. Judgment shall be pronounced publicly but the press and public may be excluded from all or part of the trial.*]" It should also be noted that European Court of Human Rights stated in its judgement that the CAS system is sufficiently independent and impartial, that is, in terms of its procedures for the selection and appointment of arbitrators and also, here upholding the case argued by the applicant, that the absence of a public hearing in "*less serious*" cases may not be incompatible with Article 6(1) of the ECHR, but will be incompatible with that provision in civil cases, in which the public nature of the hearing is fundamental and important.

Even more recently, the European Court of Human Rights again decided on an issue regarding sports justice (Ali Riza v. Switzerland, 74989/11, Judgement of award of 13 July 2021), when it found against Turkey on the grounds of violation of Article 6 (1) of the ECHR. The European Court of Human Rights found that Messrs Riza and Akal did not have a fair and equitable trial before the Arbitration Committee of the Turkish Football Federation to the extent that the said arbitration body had structural defects, given the major influence of the members, or executives, of football clubs in the organisation and workings of the Committee. The European Court of Human Rights also held that the Turkish Football Federation had failed to take the measures necessary to protect the members of the arbitration Committee from external pressures. The independence of the Arbitration Committee was therefore threatened by the same mechanisms that Pierre de Coubertin warned could undermine sports justice, via violation of the human right to a fair and equitable hearing, as enshrined in Article 6(1) of the ECHR.

Sport and the right to peace

In his famous "Ode to Sport", Coubertin included the following text: "*O Sport, you are Peace! You promote happy relations between peoples, bringing them together in their shared devotion to a strength which is controlled, organized and self-disciplined. From you, the young worldwide learn self-respect, and thus the diversity of national qualities becomes the source of a generous and friendly rivalry. Ode to Sport." Georges Hohrod and M. Eschbach (Coubertin's pseudonym, 1912)*. Peace between nations was always a priority for Pierre de Coubertin, who believed that sport was an important engine of peace, and a rapid and effective means for the development of the individual, and of communication and understanding between peoples.

Coubertin based his humanitarian and progressive view of society in general, and sport in particular, on his conviction that there is an absolute need to promote mutual understanding between peoples, as a fundamental premise of a peace project. For Coubertin, respect presupposes mutual understanding and facilitates fraternity between peoples, that is, peoples only have mutual respect when they know each other. This rapprochement operates as a means to discard exaggerated nationalism and chauvinism, to mitigate disputes, to eliminate misunderstandings and war between nations, and to attenuate rage and rancour.

Coubertin never doubted the need for each nation to know the history of other nations, and saw this as the essential basis of the educational process necessary for mutual understanding. However, the Baron knew that this was not enough, because understanding also presupposes encounter, direct contact between people who belong to different peoples, and the sharing of experience, in an international context, on the basis of equality. Accordingly, there was a need for a means to bring peoples together, on the basis of internationalism and egalitarianism. Coubertin discovered this means. He founded the Olympic Games of the Modern Era, a four-yearly worldwide event that would bring together the citizens of the entire world, particularly young people, and be an ideal institutionalised platform and event for a worldwide process of education for peace.

As the Olympic Games are the apex of this educational process, it is natural that sport would play a significant role in the preparation of the event, and would gradually assume a twofold pacificatory role, involving the pacification of relations between social classes, on the one hand, and the pacification of relations between countries, on the other. In other words, Coubertin found in sport, the seed needed to obtain both social peace and international peace. It is therefore easy to understand Coubertin's desire that the Holy Truce, or Olympic Truce, of the Olympic era should be revived, proclaimed, honoured and respected, in accordance with the four-yearly Olympic cycle. Coubertin viewed the Olympic Truce as "*an essential aspect of Olympism*", which is associated with the idea of a cycle,[25] a sort of temporary cessation of quarrels, disputes and misunderstandings, and that this type of *negative peace*, or armistice, or bellic interval, gives rise to a *positive* conception of peace linked to an uninterrupted and long-term structured peace project.[26] However, and even if the significance of the Ancient Truce was somewhat different, it nevertheless impressed Coubertin, and his interpretation of it strengthened the institution he founded, and gave it a guarantee taken from the ancient past.[27]

For all these reasons, Pierre de Coubertin was a major peace activist and a representative of the European Movement for Peace, whose name was even suggested for the Nobel Peace Prize.

Pierre de Coubertin was the fundamental source of the idea that peace should be enshrined in the Olympic Charter, as transcribed earlier, as an objective of Olympism. Likewise, the mission and role of the IOC as stated in Rule 2(4) of *the Olympic Charter* requires the IOC to cooperate with the proper public and private authorities in order to place sport at the service of humanity, and therefore promote peace. The provisions in the Olympic Charter regarding the composition and general structure of the Olympic Movement also establish that the education of young people via sport practised in accordance with Olympism, and its values, is a way to build a better and more peaceful world, and an objective of Olympism.

Sport can undoubtedly play a significant role in the promotion of peace, which is also an objective of the UN: "*To practice tolerance and live in peace*" are objectives in the Charter of the United Nations,[28] which provides that *"All Members shall settle their international disputes by peaceful means in such a manner that international peace and security, and justice, are not endangered*" (Article 3 (3)). The "Declaration on the Right of Peoples to Peace", which was adopted by the UN General Assembly on 12 November 1984, by Resolution 39/11, solemnly proclaimed that "*the peoples of our planet have a sacred right to peace*", and that states are required to take appropriate measures towards that end, at the national and international levels, is also very relevant.

Curiously, and as a practical example of this intersection between sport and peace, the UN General Meeting has, since 1993, approved Resolutions that call for compliance with the Olympic Truce (Resolution no. 48/11, 25 October 1993), the most recent of which was approved in the context of the 2020 Tokyo Olympic Games (Building a peaceful and better world through sport and the Olympic ideal: resolution/adopted by the General Assembly, Un General Assembly, 74th Session: 2019–2020, 2019). This was even referred to expressly in the famous UN Millennium Declaration, in 2000 (Point 11–10), which urges, "*Member States to observe the Olympic Truce, individually and collectively, now and in the future, and to support the International Olympic Committee in its efforts to promote peace and human understanding through sport and the Olympic Ideal*".

In short, sport, in its role in the promotion of peace and amicable relations between states, teaches values such as tolerance, friendship, mutual understanding and equality, and is a didactic paradigm for the development of a democratic culture, which is characterised by solidarity and respect for fundamental ethical principles.[29] Sport is therefore an excellent tool in the search for peace, understanding between peoples and nations, respect, tolerance and mutual aid and is therefore an important way to promote the right to peace, which is a typical third-generation right. All in continuation of the path blazed by Pierre de Coubertin with the five rings, many white doves and with the scales of justice in his hand.

Notes

1 This chapter (with a few modifications) was firstly published in the Diagoras Journal: www.diagorasjournal.com/index.php/diagoras/article/view/130/78.
2 *Pierre de Coubertin*, Fayat, 1988, page 13.
3 Monique BERLIOUX, *The International Olympic Committee*, Report of the Tenth Session of the IOA at Olympia, Athens, IOA, 1970, page 2.
4 See http://gddc.ministeriopublico.pt/pagina/o-que-sao-os-direitos-humanos.
5 "Lecture transversale des textes relatifs aux droits de l'Homme appliqués au sport", in *Sports et garanties fondamentales: Violences -dopage*, Ed. KORCHIA, Nathalie and PETTITI, Christophe, Institut de Formation en Droits de l´Homme du Barreau de Paris, 2003, page 47.
6 "Olympisme et droits de l'Homme", in *Revue Juridique et Économique du Sport*, Paris, 2008, page 143.
7 Jean MORANGE, "Sport et Droits de l'Homme", in *Revue Juridique et Économique du Sport*, Paris, 1992, page 6.
8 James A.R. NAFZIGER, *International Sports Law*, 2nd Edition, 2004, pages 130–131.
9 Robert DAVIS, "Olympic Competition: An Opportunity to Participate or a Privilege with Obligations", in *Sports & European Community Law: International Applications*, Ed. D. PANAGIOTOPOULOS, Athens, ION Publishing Group, 1997, page 157.
10 "Sobre la práctica del deporte como derecho humano", *JURI-AGE Red Tiempo de los Derechos Número 31*, Año 2018, ISNN:1989-8797, pages 2–3.
11 *Pierre de Coubertin: La deuxième croisade – Améliorer la condition humaine par le sport et l'éducation, facteurs de paix universelle*, Mussée Olympique Lausanne, Histoires et Faits, 1996, page 10.
12 Haut Commissariat aux droits de l'homme (OHCR): *Tous les sports pour tous, Le Comité Internationale Olympique et le système des Nations Unies: Pour l'édification d'un monde pacifique et meilleur grâce au sport et à l'idéal Olympique*, CIO, Lausanne, 2002, page 66.
13 *Pierre de Coubertin 1863–1937 Olimpismo- Seleção de textos*, Comité Internacional Pierre de Coubertin, Edit. Norbert MÜLLER and Nelson Schneider TODT, ediPUCRS, Porto Alegre, 2015, pages 581–582.
14 Peter DONNELY, "Sport and human rights", in *Sport in Society*, Volume 11, 2008, Issue 4: Sport and Foreign Policy in a Globalizing World, page 42.
15 Alberto SCAVARELLI, "Human Rights and Sport", in *Sport, Ethique, Culture: Human Rights. Society. Olympic Movement*, Ed. Antonio DAINO, Azienda Grafica Busco – Rapallo/Panathlon Internacional, 2003, page 280.
16 See André SENAY and Robert HERNET, *Monsieur de Coubertin*, Paris, 1956, page 58.
17 See, Richard D. MANDELL, *Las Primeras Olimpiadas Modernas – Atenas, 1896*, Barcelona, Ediciones bellatterra, 1990, page 61.
18 See Antonio LOMBARDO, "Pierre de Coubertin visto da vicino", in *Religio athletae – Pierre de Coubertin e la formazione dell'uomo per la*

società complessa, Ed. R. FRASCA, Rome, Società Stampa Sportiva, 2007, pages 52–53.

19 UN, CDN, General Observation no. 17 (2013, para 14 d & 58 g).

20 UN CDN, General Observation no. 15 (2013), para 4.

21 No reference.

22 "A Prática do Exercício Físico e o Desporto de Participação: um Princípio do Estado Democrático de Direito para Concretizar o Direito Fundamental à Saúde na Sociedade Brasileira", in *Direito Desportivo: Transdisciplinariedade e Autonomia*, Org. ÂNGELO VARGAS, Belo Horizonte, Casa da Educação Física, March 2022, page 10.

23 *Pierre de Coubertin 1863–1937 Olimpismo-Seleção de Textos*, Ed. Norbert MÜLLER and Nelson S. TODT, ediPUCRS, Porto Alegre, 2015, page 656.

24 *Pierre de Coubertin 1863–1937 Olimpismo-Seleção de Textos*, Ed. Norbert MÜLLER and Nelson S. TODT, ediPUCRS, Porto Alegre, 2015, page 670.

25 Jean DURRY, *Le vraie Pierre de Coubertin: La vie, L'œuvre, Les textes-clés*, Paris, Comité Français Pierre de Coubertin, 1994, page 43.

26 Antonella STELITANO, *Le Olimpiadi all'ONU – Le Nazioni Unite e lo Sport: dall'embargo all'Olimpismo*, CLEUP SC – "Coop. Libraria Editrice Università di Padova", Padova, 2012, page 67.

27 Françoise ÉTIENNE and Roland ÉTIENNE, "Les Jeux Olympiques en Grèce 776 av. J-C. 1896–2004", in *Dossiers d'Arquéologie* no. 294, Juin 2004, page 56.

28 Jean DURRY, *op. cit.*, page 43.

29 Andrés FERNÁNDEZ DIÁZ and José Andrés FERNÁNDEZ CORNEJO, "Derechos Humanos y economia del bienstar: Una reflexión", in *La Declaración Universal de los Derechos Humanos en su 50 aniversario*, Barcelona, Ed. Bosch, 1999, page 645.

5 The meaning and scope of sport as a human right as enshrined in the Olympic Charter

The meaning and scope of sport as a (human) right as enshrined in the Olympic Charter

In the August 2021 version of the Olympic Charter, the Fourth Fundamental Principle of the Olympic Charter reads as follows: "*The practice of sport is a human right. Every individual must have the possibility of practising sport, without discrimination of any kind and in the Olympic spirit, which requires mutual understanding with a spirit of friendship, solidarity and fair play.*"

This Principle was slightly altered for the current version of the Olympic Charter, adopted at the 141st Session of the International Olympic Committee, in Mumbai, India, in October 2023. The text now reads as follows: *"The practice of sport is a human right. Every individual must have* ***access to the practice*** *of sport, without discrimination of any kind* ***in respect of internationally recognised human rights within the remit of the Olympic Movement****. The Olympic spirit requires mutual understanding with a spirit of friendship, solidarity and fair play"* (emphasis added).

The amended text retains the statement that sport is a human right. We agree with this option, in line with the approach of Pierre COLLOMB,[1] who argues that sport is a human activity in the full sense of the term, because, in it, man puts his most precious asset, that is, his body, into play. The truth is that this approach is unparalleled in any other binding international human rights instrument, such as the Universal Declaration of Human Rights, or the European Convention on Human Rights. Although the statement that sport is a human right is copied almost word for word, in Article 1 of the UNESCO International Charter of Physical Education and Sport, UNESCO, which is titled: "*The practice of physical education, physical activity and sport is a fundamental right for all*", particularly in paragraph 1 thereof: *"Every human being has a fundamental right to physical education, physical activity and sport without discrimination on the basis of ethnicity, gender, sexual orientation, language, religion, political or other opinion, national or social origin, property or any other basis."*

DOI: 10.4324/9781003569749-7

Secondly, it is evident that the legislator wanted to stress the nature of this personal right, which cannot be viewed as a mere possibility, or as something hypothetical, or potential, but must be effective, via guaranteed access to sport activity.

There is also a reference to human rights, as recognised internationally, combined with a link with the Olympic Movement. In this way, the IOC, acting via a Fundamental Principle of the Olympic Charter, manages to impose human rights as recognised in Public International Law, that is, human rights as enshrined in international legal instruments adopted by States, on the various constituent parts of the Olympic Movement, via their obligation to comply fully with the Olympic Charter (cf. the Seventh Fundamental Principle of Olympism, and Rule 1.4, both in the Olympic Charter). In this context, access to sport activity must be ensured in a manner that also complies with other human rights, as enshrined in international human rights law.

We also consider that the express and limitative reference to the Olympic Movement has another objective. For by encapsulating the right to sport within the context of the Olympic Movement, the persons addressed by the right are players and athletes involved in competitive federation sport, within the Olympic pyramid with the IOC and the Olympic Games at its apex, immediately above the international sports federations, and the National Olympic Committees, which are the three main constituent parts of the Olympic Movement.

For example, consider the definition of the Olympic Movement in the Third Fundamental Principle of Olympism: "***The Olympic Movement is*** *the concerted, organised, universal and permanent action, carried out under the supreme authority of the IOC, of all individuals and entities who are inspired by the values of Olympism. It covers the five continents. It reaches its peak with the bringing together of the world's athletes at the great sports festival, the Olympic Games. Its symbol is five interlaced rings*" (emphasis added).

The Fifth Principle also refers to the Olympic Movement as an overall framework of organised sport: "*Recognising that sport occurs within the framework of society, sports organisations* ***within the Olympic Movement***" (emphasis added).

This is also evident from the said Seventh Fundamental Principle, which refers to a relationship of membership, which arises on recognition by the IOC: "*Belonging to the* ***Olympic Movement*** *requires compliance with the Olympic Charter and recognition by the IOC*" (emphasis added).

Rule 1 of the Olympic Charter ("*Composition and general organisation of the Olympic Movement*") is even clearer regarding the fact that the Olympic Movement comprises a federative pyramid, with the athletes and players at its base, and the IOC at its apex. This rule is therefore transcribed in full below, given its relevance to the topic of this chapter:

> *1. Under the supreme authority and leadership of the International Olympic Committee, the Olympic Movement encompasses organisations,*

> *athletes and other persons who agree to be guided by the Olympic Charter. The goal of the Olympic Movement is to contribute to building a peaceful and better world by educating youth through sport practised in accordance with Olympism and its values.*
>
> *2. The three main constituents of the Olympic Movement are the International Olympic Committee ("IOC"), the International Sport federations ("IFs") and the National Olympic Committees ("NOCs").*
>
> *3. In addition to its three main constituents, the Olympic Movement also encompasses the Organising Committees for the Olympic Games ("OCOGs"), the national associations, clubs and persons belonging to the IFs and NOCs, particularly the athletes, whose interests constitute a fundamental element of the Olympic Movement's action, as well as the judges, referees, coaches and the other sports officials and technicians. It also includes other organisations and institutions as recognised by the IOC.*
>
> *4. Any person or organisation belonging in any capacity whatsoever to the Olympic Movement is bound by the provisions of the Olympic Charter and shall abide by the decisions of the IOC.*

It is therefore necessary to draw the following conclusion, that is, when the Olympic Charter proclaims the right to sport, as a human right, it does so solely in relation to competitive, organised and federation sport.

However, there is another aspect to be considered regarding the meaning and scope of the inclusion of the right to sport in the Olympic Charter, as a human right, on the basis of a systematic interpretation of the Fourth Fundamental Principle of Olympism, transcribed earlier. This aspect concerns the fact that the IOC includes access to sport activity, as a human right, equality, in the sense of non-discrimination, and sport ethics (in the allusion made to the Olympic spirit and fair play) in the Fourth Fundamental Principle, which is identical to the approach adopted by UNESCO, and also similar to the approach of the Council of Europe[2] and the European Commission.[3]

The IOC urges the Olympic Movement to adopt rules and to work to ensure access to sport activity, free of all discrimination.

The IOC is the body primarily subject to a duty to comply with the principle of equality, in the sense of non-discrimination, for example, in the definition and establishment of the criteria for the selection of the sports to be included in the Olympic Programme, or of cities to host the Olympic Games.

For example, the International Sports Federations are required, as another of the three main constituent parts of the Olympic Movement, to act in accordance with objective, non-arbitrary and non-discriminatory criteria, in the exercise of their power under the Olympic Charter to fix the age limits for the competitions in each sport (Rule 42 of the Olympic Charter). Likewise, international sports federations are required to comply with the principle of equality, that is, non-discrimination, in the definition of the technical rules governing the various sports (Rule 6.1 and the By-Law to Rule 33 of the

Olympic Charter). [It is noted that one of the aspects under consideration, in high-profile cases, such as the Semenya case (access of an intersex athlete to competitive sport) or the Oscar Pistorius case (simultaneous access to the Olympic Games and the Paralympics by an athlete with prostheses that replace amputated legs), in which the IAAF eligibility rules were at issue, was precisely the principle of equality, that is, non-discrimination.]

The provisions of the Olympic Charter regarding the National Olympic Committees include a provision, which seeks to prevent unfounded discrimination that prevents those with sporting merit from competing in the Olympic Games, that is, Paragraph 4 of Rule 44 ("*Invitations and entries*"), which provides that "*An NOC shall only enter competitors upon the recommendations for entries given by national federations. If the NOC approves thereof, it shall transmit such entries to the OCOG. The OCOG must acknowledge their receipt. NOCs must investigate the validity of the entries proposed by the national federations and <u>ensure that no one has been excluded for racial, religious or political reasons or by reason of other forms of discrimination</u>*" (emphasis added).

The dual approach described, which ensures, on the one hand, that athletes are entitled to participate in competitions, and on the other, that their participation is subject to the prior confirmation of the equality of all competitors is reinforced by the IOC in *Implementing Provision of the IOC Code of Ethics – Basic Universal Principles of Good Governance within the Olympic Movement. In Principle 5* ("*Support to Athletes*"), paragraph 5.1. ("*Athletes' rights and responsibilities*") provides as follows:

> *Appropriate measures should be taken to adopt and implement the Athletes' Rights and Responsibilities Declaration.*
>
> *The right of athletes to participate in sports competitions and within applicable rules including competition laws) shall be protected.*
>
> *No form of discrimination on whatever grounds, be it race, colour, sex, sexual, orientation, language, religion, political or other opinion, national or social origin, property, birth or other status, shall be tolerated.*

The *"Athletes' Rights and Responsibilities Declaration"* was adopted in 2018. This declaration does make express reference to a right to sport, but refers to the capacity and opportunity of athletes and players to take part in sport, free of all discrimination:

> *This Declaration aspires to promote the ability and opportunity of athletes to:*
>
> 1. *Practise sport and compete without being subject to discrimination on the basis of race, colour, religion, age, sex, sexual orientation, disability, language, political or other opinion, national or social origin, property, birth or other immutable status.*

It is noted that the source of the idea of an "*opportunity*" to compete, rather than a right to compete, may be the United States of America,[4] where it was decided that there is no right to compete in organised sports competitions, and where Congress declined to legislate a right of athletes to compete internationally, but instead opted to establish an "*opportunity*" to compete.[5] This option was adopted when Congress was called on to counterpose the rights of athletes to choose the sport in which they wish to compete, and "*organisational rights*", that is, the right to determine the eligibility of athletes, or players, or of the team to which they belong, to compete in a competition,[6] that is, factors such as age, weight, and amateur, or professional, status, and obviously the performance of the athlete or player.[7]

This approach is in line with an arbitration award of the Court of Arbitration for Sport in Lausanne, which could not now be so assertive, in the light of the bolstering of the text of the Fourth Fundamental Principle of the Olympic Charter. In a case in September 2000,[8] in which the Panel decided that "*There is no rule of 'fairness', to be derived from the Olympic Charter's acknowledgement that the practice of sport is a fundamental human right, which would under such circumstances create an outer time limit of Olympic ineligibility.*"

We consider that the approach that should now be adopted, in accordance with the Olympic Charter, is that access to competitive sport under the auspices of the Olympic Movement, and the conduct of competitive sport should be viewed as a human right. However, the implementation of the principle of equality, that is, non-discrimination, and sport ethics will converge to ensure not only that athletes' access to competitions is not restricted, other than for objective reasons, but also that athletes will not be authorised to compete in competitions, when they have an a priori competitive advantage in relation to the other competitors. [This is not the place to consider the merits of the access of transsexual and transgender athletes and players to sport competitions, however, we note that when the issue is considered solely in terms of human rights, such athletes and players should always be guaranteed access to competitive sport, and that failure to do so amounts to discrimination. However, it may be necessary, in the name of sport ethics, and in order to prevent unjustified positive discrimination, to prohibit, or restrict, their access to competitive sport]. It is of fundamental importance to ensure that merit is always the primary and prevailing consideration in the definition of eligibility rules, but always without discrimination.

The decision of the IOC Ethics Committee, dated 21 October 2003, is a classic example of what could be a good decision in circumstances related to the right to sport. The matter at issue in that case was a decision of the Board of Management of the International Volleyball Federation of 6 May 2003, which had suspended the Argentine Volleyball Federation. The result of this decision was that the Argentinian players were excluded from various competitions, including world competitions, without having committed any offence, as the reasons for the suspension were wholly attributable to acts of management of the Argentine Volleyball Federation. Moreover, the International Volleyball Federation, after having prohibited the beach volleyball players, subsequently authorised them to compete in competitions because they were professional players, but upheld the exclusion of indoor volleyball players from competitions, because they were amateurs.

The Ethics Committee held in its decision that the right to sport recognised in the Olympic Charter cannot be confused with the notion of "sport for all", but nevertheless applies to international high-level, or high-performance, sport. The Ethics Committee also noted that the Fundamental Principles of the Olympic Charter do not confer an unconditional right to participate in competitions, and that each international sports federation may restrict the right to participate in its competitions, subject to the proviso that this restriction must not be contrary to the Fundamental Principles,[9] and provided that the sport activity is free of discrimination.

The Ethics Committee accordingly decided in summary that (i) the suspension of players was a violation of their right to participate in international competitions and (ii) that the fact that some players were banned from international competitions on the basis that they were amateurs was unjustified discrimination.

It can therefore be seen from this decision that the right to sport, enshrined in the Olympic Charter as a human right, is not an absolute right: firstly, and because its subjective scope is limited to the constituent parts of the Olympic Movement, it is above all a right that concerns the access and eligibility conditions adopted by sport federations,[10] which must not be discriminatory, and secondarily, because the validity of these eligibility conditions must be evaluated in accordance with Sport ethics, in order to avoid improper competitive advantages.

However, the application of the right to sport is not limited to eligibility rules but also extends to disciplinary penalties imposed for doping, which, like eligibility rules, also prevent athletes and players from competing. Athletes and players, who violate the anti-doping rules, are punished because of a violation of sport ethics, and in order to defend public health. This punishment can involve suspension for extended periods, and even lifetime bans, when this is permitted by the relevant legal system (although not in Portugal). An athlete, or player, who is suspended, or subject to a lifetime ban, suffers a restriction, or even complete prohibition of the exercise of the right to sport. This is because this human right is not absolute. Indeed, the preamble of the World Anti-Doping Code states that one of the aims of the Code and of the World Anti-Doping Programme is *"to protect the Athletes' fundamental right to participate in doping-free sport and thus promote health, fairness and equality for Athletes worldwide*". The right to sport is a fundamental right, but it is subject to the existence of justice and equality between competing athletes and players.

The key to the human right to sport is therefore in the hands of sports organisations, particularly international sports organisations, and in the way they consider the creation and adoption of the rules governing sport, within the overall framework of the Olympic Movement.

Notes

1 "Lecture transversale des textes relatifs aux droits de l'homme appliqués au sport", in *Sport et Garanties Fondamentales: Violence – Dopage*, Coord. Nathalie KORCHA e C. PETTITI, Institut de Formation en Droits de l'Homme du Barreau de Paris, 2003, page 47.

2 Article 10 of the 2021 European Sport Charter concerns precisely the "The right to sport" and number 1 covers precisely access for all: "*Access to sport for all is considered to be a fundamental right. All human beings have an inalienable right of access to sport in a safe environment, both inside and outside school settings, which is essential for their personal development and instrumental in the exercise of the rights to health, education, culture and participation in the life of the community.*" Paragraph 2 contains a reference to non-discrimination: "*No discrimination on the grounds of race, colour, language, religion, gender or sexual orientation, political or other opinion, national or social origin, association with a national minority, property, birth or other status, shall be permitted in the access to sports facilities or to sports activities.*"

3 "*Sport involves all citizens regardless of gender, race, age, disability, religion and belief, sexual orientation and social or economic background.*" – White Paper on Sport, Brussels, 11.7.2007 COM(2007) 391 final.

4 Cf. James A.R. NAFZIGER, *International Sports Law*, 2nd Edition, 2004, pages 130–131.

5 Cf. James A.R. NAFZIGER, *International Sports Law*, 2nd Edition, 2004, page 324.

6 Cf. Robert DAVIS, "Olympic Competition: An Opportunity to Participate or a Privilege with Obligations", in *Sports & European Community Law: International Implications*, Ed. D. PANAGIOTOPOULOS, Atenas, ION Publishing Group, 1997, page 157.

7 It is the athletes and players themselves who prioritise performance and sporting merit. Cf. Article 2 of the Universal Declaration of Players Rights, adopted by the World Players Association: "Every player has the right to access and pursue sport as a career and profession based solely on merit."

8 Arbitration in the CAS ad hoc Division, at the Sydney Olympic Games, Case 00/001, *USOC and USA Canoe/Kayak -v- IOC*, judgement of 13 September 2000, § 26.

9 CAS no. 3/03, *ODEPA/PASO -v- FIVB*, judgement of 21 October 2013.

10 Lydie COHEN, *Le droit au sport des personnes en situation de handicap*, Thèse de doctorat, Université de Limoges. Cf. Presented and defended on 9 December 2022 – copy kindly provided by the author.

6 Sports and religious freedom

A legal perspective

Background

Contemporary society is based on multiculturalism, secularisation and a multiplicity of opinions and beliefs of individuals and groups. There are various traditional religions: Judaism, Christianity, Islam, Confucianism, Taoism, Hinduism, and their variants, some of which are based on texts, or compilations of texts, such as the Torah, the Bible or the Koran. This gives rise to a religious order, *"the role of this order is to govern the human conduct of individuals, who profess the same faith, both in their relationships with each other, and in their relationship with God. This order is therefore an order of transcendences, or faith."*[1] In addition to a moral order, there is also legal order, of which the Law of the Catholic Church and Canon Law are living examples.[2] This can easily be explained given the role of law in the regulation of social phenomena.

Sport is another social reality in the contemporary global village, which has a major impact on people's lives. In sport, citizens, supporters, support different clubs, and national teams, in an equally multicultural context. Sport is also a social phenomenon in which law has a role, and gives rise to a sport legal order, that is, Sport Law.

The relationship between sport and religious freedom is one of the many issues that arise regarding the relationship between law and sport, and the issue we shall consider summarily in this chapter.

Religious freedom

Portugal is a secular state, in which religious pluralism is recognised, Church and State are separated, and in which the principle of the non-confessional nature of the state applies. However, this does not mean that the Portuguese legal order is indifferent to the religious order. The most significant confirmation of this is the fact that the Constitution and the law guarantee religious freedom.[3] Article 41 of the Constitution of the Portuguese Republic enshrines "*freedom of conscience, religion, and worship*". There is also a "Law of

DOI: 10.4324/9781003569749-8

Religious Freedom", Law No 16/2001, of 22 June. With this underlying legal framework, the Portuguese state does not prevent anyone from professing a certain belief, and entitles those who follow a certain religion to fulfil their religious obligations, in terms of worship, family and education. However, the Portuguese state neither imposes nor provides a legal guarantee of the performance of these duties.[4]

Concomitantly, religious freedom is also the subject matter of various international instruments that protect human rights.[5]

However, what do we mean when we refer to freedom of religion, or religious freedom? Religious freedom is "*one of the fundamental rights of a democratic society, and must be understood in a broad manner, to include theistic, non-theistic, and atheistic positions, and the right not to adopt any religion*".[6] Accordingly, religious freedom includes the coexistence *of the "freedom to have of neutral spaces, secular spaces"*, "*multi-religious spaces*", and "*spaces free of tension (or pathos)*".[7] "*Religious freedom protects the right of every individual to profess, express, practise, or change, their religious beliefs, either individually, or in conjunction with other individuals, and also protects the personal nature of these beliefs, and prohibits any discrimination because of them.*"[8] In the wake of the case law of the European Court of Human Rights (ECtHR), religious freedom is a cement of democratic society, an essential freedom that protects the identity and beliefs of believers, atheists, agnostics and sceptics, and those who are merely indifferent. All are protected by the right to religious freedom, which ensures pluralism, and includes the freedom to change religion, the freedom to continue to profess a religion and the freedom to express a religion.

Religious freedom protects an internal, or passive, aspect, and an external, or active, aspect. The internal or passive aspect (*forum internum*), which is also termed freedom of belief, is the freedom to adopt, or not to adopt, a belief, and is associated with the individual's conviction, profession of faith, credo, and personal beliefs. This is the most intimate aspect of belief, and intellectual self-determination regarding religion, which is linked to the personhood and dignity of the individual.[9] The external, or active, aspect (*forum externum*), which is also termed freedom of worship, is the freedom to express the belief adopted. This expression can be individual or collective (community worship). Religious freedom therefore also involves the freedom of religious confessions, as reflected in the external acts that demonstrate devotion to a particular religion, for example, ceremonies (such as communion) and rites (such as circumcision or baptism). It should also be noted that "*almost all religions require believers to practice their religion, in addition to mere belief*",[10] and that "while *some more contemplative religions only require prayer, others require social action.*"[11]

It should be noted that religious freedom is not an absolute freedom. It is subject to some restrictions, in exceptional circumstances, which are solely related to its external aspects. This means that individuals are not always entitled to conduct themselves in accordance with their religious beliefs. Accordingly, and on the basis of Article 9 of the European Convention on Human Rights (ECHR), the restriction of external aspects of religious freedom is subject to the following preconditions: (i) the restriction must be provided in the law, in order to avoid arbitrary impositions, that is, the restriction must be substantive, and not merely formal. Such provisions include bylaws, administrative regulations, case law and even unwritten law; (ii) the restriction must fulfil a legitimate purpose, via the reconciliation of individual rights and the public interest, for example, public security, policy and morality and (iii) the restriction must be necessary in a democratic society, and be proportionate to the objective pursued (test of proportionality). These are therefore the preconditions that must be complied with when a particular sport rule, or activity, restricts religious freedom, that is, such restrictions must be legal, legitimate and proportionate.

Moreover, Article 14 of the ECHR, which complements Article 9 of the ECHR, enshrines the principle of non-discrimination. The right not to be discriminated against is a heteronomic right linked to the effective enjoyment of other rights recognised in the ECHR. Religious freedom is therefore inseparable from the right of all persons not to suffer direct, or indirect, discrimination, on the grounds of religion. Moreover, "*discrimination between human beings on the grounds of religion, or belief, is an affront to human dignity, and a disavowal of the principles of the Charter of the United Nations.*"[12] This inseparability should therefore also be considered when evaluating the validity of certain sports rules and activities.

Likewise, we cannot also overlook the right to education and its role in the full development of the human person, particularly, the requirement, included in various international legal instruments,[13] of understanding, tolerance and friendship between all religious groups, in view of the need to educate children for accordingly.[14]

Finally, freedom of expression, which also has an internal aspect, that is, freedom of opinion, and an external aspect, that is, freedom to express opinions, is also inseparable from religious freedom, that is, freedom to express religious opinions, based on the premise that the free practice of religion necessarily includes a concomitant freedom to manifest religious beliefs.

Sport and religious freedom

The primary international legal instruments include three fundamental aspects of the expression of religious freedom as applied to sport. The first aspect (3.1) is the implementation of religious freedom via the principle of non-discrimination; the second aspect (3.2) is the freedom of sport organisations to pursue their objects, without any religious interference, or intrusion; and the third aspect (3.3) is the limitation, or restriction, of the religious freedom of athletes and players. All these aspects converge in a single purpose, which is the religious neutrality of sport in general, and of sport organisations, and sport locations, in particular.

The implementation of religious freedom via the principle of non-discrimination

The first aspect, that is, non-discrimination on the grounds of religion, is enshrined in various international soft law texts. For example, the Council of Europe European Charter of Sport, Article 4(1) which guarantees all citizens access to "*facilities and activities*", free of discrimination on the grounds of religion. Similarly, Article 1.1.1 of the UNESCO International Charter of Physical Education and Sport provides that "*access to physical education, and sport*" cannot be denied on the basis of religion. This explains why, in Portugal, which is a signatory to these two documents, Article 2(1) of the Basic Law of Physical and Sport Activity,[15] provides, under the heading of "*Principles of universality and equality*", that all individuals are entitled to physical and sport activity, regardless of religion.

The approach is also adopted by international sports organisations. For example, the IOC, in Fundamental Principle no. 6 of the Olympic Charter,[16] provides that the rights and freedoms enshrined in the Olympic Charter are to be enjoyed without any discrimination on the grounds of religion, and requires National Olympic Committees to investigate the validity of the names of the athletes proposed by the national federations for membership of their Olympic missions/delegations, in order to ensure that no athlete is denied access to the Olympic Games for religious reasons. Finally, FIFA prohibits discrimination against countries, individuals, or groups of individuals, on the grounds of religion,[17] and punishes violation of this prohibition, by the suspension, or expulsion, of the offender.

The freedom of sports organisations to pursue their objects, without any religious interference, or intrusion

The IOC is also a paradigmatic example of the second aspect, that is, the neutrality of institutions. The Olympic Charter provides (i) that when members of the IOC take up office, they must take an oath to act independently of religious considerations,[18] and (ii) requires National Olympic Committees to act to ensure their autonomy, and to resist pressures of any nature, particularly those of a religious nature.[19] Another example can be found in the Rules of the International Volleyball Federation,[20] which require that the federation must not discriminate against individuals and nations on the grounds of religion, and must also refrain from any involvement in religious matters. It is notable that, in Portugal, the Portuguese Olympic Committee expressly enshrines its autonomy, by "*rejecting all influences*" of a religious nature[21]; and asserts that it is "*alien*" to such influences[22]; and that the Portuguese Sport Confederation defines itself as "*independent . . . of religious institutions*".[23] One of the many possible examples regarding Portuguese federations is the Portuguese Kick-boxing and Muaythai Federation,[24] which states that it is "*independent of the state, political parties, and religious institutions*".

It is therefore clear from these rules that the much-proclaimed autonomy of sports organisations in relation to governments and private entities is also expressed in terms of the absence of religious interference, or intrusion, and that sport organisations, acting in the exercise of their autonomy, adopt the principle of non-discrimination on the grounds of religion.

Limitation, or restriction, of the religious freedom of athletes and players

An issue that arises not infrequently is the resolution of conflicts between certain fundamental human rights of athletes and religious freedom, which is also a human right. The main cases concern freedom of expression (3.3.1), and the obligations of the athlete, or player, employee (3.3.2).

The conflict between religious freedom and freedom of expression

Our consideration of freedom of expression brings us back to the IOC rules, and, in this case, to the famous and controversial Rule 50 of the Olympic Charter, according to which "*No kind of demonstration or political, religious or racial propaganda is permitted in any Olympic sites, venues, or other areas.*"[25] However, the IOC also issued a statement titled "*Freedom of expression: a basic human right*",[26] during the presidency of Jacques Rogge, and stated that it represents 205 countries and territories, many of which are in conflict, and that the Games are not the place where any political or religious positions should be adopted. The IOC called for "*common sense*" in the application of this rule, and stated that it was protecting the right of athletes not to state an opinion, to which they are also entitled.

We understand that the Olympic Charter[27] provides that the international sports federations have autonomy in the administration of their respective sports. We also agree that the expression of an opinion should not be confused with propaganda or demonstrations. We also consider that this position, which seeks to ensure the religious neutrality of the Olympic Games, differs from the IOC prohibition of use of social networks by athletes and players during the London 2012 Olympic Games, in order to safeguard the sponsorships programme. Additionally, we are not unaware that the IOC has already made it clear that athletes may express themselves fully at press conferences and on the various media platforms, as these are not part of the Olympic infrastructures.[28] However, it is nevertheless true that athletes are prevented from freely expressing their religious beliefs.

Still within the ambit of freedom of expression, we take this opportunity to refer, in passing, to the famous case of the rugby player Israel Folau, a Christian, who has made trenchant homophobic comments on social media, which resulted in his dismissal on the grounds of violation of the Code of Conduct to which he was bound by his employer. The player invoked absence of due cause for the dismissal because it was based on his religion. This led to legal proceedings, which were settled on the basis of the payment of compensation to the player.[29]

Another very controversial issue is whether it is, or is not, possible to restrict the use of religious symbols by athletes and players, as these symbols are also an expression of their religion to third parties. There can be no doubt that religious symbols are an externalisation of religious belief, and that the display thereof is a public manifestation of religious freedom. It is "*necessary not to overlook the impact that the use of this symbol, which is presented as, or understood to be, a religious duty, may have on those who opt to not use it.*[30] Moreover, it is also necessary to clarify the legal basis for the prohibition, or limitation, of the use of such symbols by public and private persons."

Rule 4(5) of the Football Laws of the Game provides that the equipment of footballers, including underwear, must not show religious slogans, statements or images. Moreover, only in March 2014 did FIFA lift the ban on the wearing of turbans and Islamic scarfs (*hijabs*) at competitions, a prohibition that had prevented Iran from trying to qualify for the London 2012 Olympic Games.[31] In another case, the Quebec Soccer Foundation refused to permit Sikh players to play football, while wearing a turban, unless they also wore a helmet, which seemed to many to amount to discrimination on the grounds of religion. The prohibition of the wearing of the hijab, in basketball, lasted until May 2017, and we all remember when the Saudi athlete, Wojdan Ali Seraj Abdulrahim was prohibited from competing while wearing the hijab,[32] by the International Judo Federation, and that the judoka was only able to compete in the London 2012 Olympic Games, following diplomatic efforts that involved the IOC, the Saudi Olympic Committee and the International Judo Federation. Handball has also evolved in this area, and currently permits the wearing of a headscarf, provided that it is made of flexible and elastic material, but forbids the use of a scarf around the neck, or a necklace, for safety reasons.[33] In volleyball, the Board of the FIVB made a decision on 18 March 2012 for immediate implementation, which altered the rules regarding the clothing of female beach volleyball players, in order to respect religious customs and beliefs. The 1988 Indian motor vehicle legislation regarding motor vehicles, which exempts turban-wearing Sikhs from wearing crash helmets, is a further example of this trend.[34]

This brings us to two almost identical judgements of the ECtHR against France, that is, the Dogru case[35] and the Osmanoglu and Kocabas case.[36]

The former case is a paradigmatic example of the difficulties involved in balancing respect for diversity in religious matters, the welfare (or overriding interests) of a child,[37] and the integration and socialisation role of the public school system. In that case, 11-year-old Belgin Dogru, who was registered in the first year of secondary education, refused to remove her Islamic veil in Physical Education classes, despite successive instructions of the teacher to do so.

This refusal amounted to violation of a rule in a school regulation, which had been communicated on registration, and which required removal of the Islamic headscarf/veil during the Physical Education classes. The French government acknowledged that the rule interfered with the student's right to express her religious beliefs in public, but considered that the requirements of Article 9(2) of the ECHR were met: that is, legality, legitimacy and proportionality. According to the French government, the legitimate objectives of the rule included the safeguarding of the rights and freedoms of all students, avoidance of negative effects on colleagues prevention of the disruption of lessons; protection of good order, and ensuring of student compliance with the duty to wear appropriate clothing compatible with the normal conduct of classes. The French government also invoked reasons of public health and safety; and the need to prevent the student's conduct from challenging the public education system per se.

The ECtHR accepted the arguments of the French government and stressed the need to respect the secularism of the French public school system, and the fact that the prohibition was not absolute because it was limited to Physical Education classes. The ECtHR decided that there was no violation of Article 9 of the ECHR, and that the use of an Islamic headscarf/veil may be incompatible with sport, strictly for reasons of safety, or hygiene, and that the penalty imposed was nothing more than a consequence of the students' refusal to comply with the rules in force in the school, of which they had been fully informed, at all times.

We consider that there can be no doubt that the use of a veil is the manifestation of a religion, and that a public school must respect the secular nature of the state, that is, the religious neutrality of the state. We also consider that physical education is, per se, neutral, and involves neither religious dogmas nor religious thought. It is also clear that children must comply with their duty to attend classes regularly, and that there is a need to accommodate the duty to attend school and the manifestation of religion. We also agree that there should be standard rules regarding sports equipment, for the sake of equality, to ensure the use of sport-appropriate clothing, and in order not to prejudice the normal conduct of activities or the educational content of the lesson.[38] However, we do not consider that the use of a veil would amount to a threat to the health, hygiene or public safety of the student and/or her colleagues. Likewise, we do not consider that the use of a veil would create a climate of tension between the student and her colleagues, as it does not amount to an attempt to convert, or influence, other students, which could give rise to a public policy issue, or to a threat to peace between religions. While we consider that the creation of minority religious groups in schools is to be avoided, particularly in order to prevent the marginalisation of religious minorities, we do not consider that this could be the result of wearing a veil in a specific lesson. Moreover, the context of these cases was Physical Education, and not a competitive context in which the standardisation of equipment is vital. Accordingly, and in the light of the grounds of Article 9(2) of the ECHR, we believe that this case involves a disproportionate restriction of the religious freedom of the student, as the veil is undoubtedly an integral part of her identity, her personality and her relationship with God, and that the obligation in question does not amount to an urgent social need.

We open a brief parenthesis at this point in the discussion of the issue of freedom of expression, to note that we consider that this case could also be considered in terms of non-discrimination, and equality between men and women. The right of individuals to dress as they wish is not one of the fundamental freedoms, but religious freedom is protected. Accordingly, if a particular item of clothing is only used by women, it is also necessary to consider their freedom, as women, to express their religion and their beliefs, either individually, or in a group, in public or private, through worship, teaching, practices and rituals.[39] [40]

Without prejudice to our view regarding this particular case, we nevertheless wish to stress that we comprehend that in certain sports, such as karting, and other motor sports, the wearing of a crucifix, or rosary, can be unsafe. We also agree with rules, such as the rule in basketball that prohibits the use of helmets, hair adornments, or jewellery, that are sharp, or a hazard to the physical integrity of the athletes, in a context of intense, inevitable and repeated physical contact. In these situations, we consider that the violation of religious freedom is objectively justified, provided that there is no other method that is less restrictive of religious freedom. However, it will always be necessary to apply the proportionality test, as the Ontario Human Rights Court did in the case of the boxer, Pardeep Nagra, who was confronted with a regulatory ban on bearded boxers, imposed by the Canadian Amateur Boxing Association. This boxer refused to comply with the rule, because his beard was part of his religious beliefs, and as much a religious practice, or rite, as is the wearing of a turban, or veil. The Court ordered the inclusion of the boxer in the contest in question, provided that he covered his beard. The Ontario Supreme Court subsequently upheld the finding that the provision at issue was incompatible with the human rights principles consolidated in Canadian law, and with the Canadian Charter of Rights and Freedoms.[41] It is therefore concluded that recourse to less restrictive measures may indeed involve the use of equipment adapted for the sport, such as has been developed by brands like Nike and Adidas, which "*have developed sport clothing that enable women to wear clothes with a modern and female cut, without violating religious precepts*".[42]

We shall now consider the case of *Osmanoglu and Kocabas*,[43] in which the applicants (Swiss Muslim citizens of Turkish origin, who are also Turkish nationals, resident in Basle, Switzerland) commenced legal proceedings to challenge the fact that their two Muslim daughters registered in a public school were required to take the mixed swimming lessons included in the school curriculum (as part of Physical Education), as part of compulsory education. The children's parents considered that the said obligation was contrary to their religious beliefs, and further that the fine imposed on them for failure to comply with the said obligation had neither a basis in law nor a legitimate purpose, and was therefore disproportionate.

The ECtHR noted that the objective of social integration pursued by activities such as swimming classes is fundamental, and prevails over considerations regarding development and health, and also cannot give way to the parents' religious beliefs. According to the ECtHR, the idea is that a state may impose duties on individuals that directly contradict their beliefs, and may restrict religious freedom in order to achieve a legitimate purpose, that is, when the reason is to support foreign children, with cultural and religious differences, and to integrate them in the school, in accordance with compulsory education, and for reasons of gender equality, in order to ensure that all students receive the same education. According to the ECtHR, "A *child's interest in attending those lessons lies not merely in learning to swim and taking physical exercise, but above all in participating in that activity with all the other pupils, without exception on the basis of the child's origin or the parents' religious or philosophical convictions*."

Moreover, there was an effort to ensure proportionality in this case. According to the ECtHR, the authorities demonstrated an excellent balancing of the principles, rights and interests, in play, as the authorities authorised the children to use a burkini during Physical Education lessons, to dress away from boys, to avoid any promiscuity, or indecent exposure,[44] and managed to achieve a compromise between the obligation imposed by the French State Educational Programme, that the children must attend lessons, on the one hand, and the children's right to religious freedom, on the other.

Furthermore, the authorities were also able to ensure the parents' right to ensure that their children receive an education that is in accordance with their religion,[45] under Article 2 of Protocol 1 to the ECHR, which protects the parents' right, as the persons legally responsible for their children's education, to an education that respects their religious beliefs. The dynamic that must exist is one of educational pluralism. For, while the state must be able to formulate its educational programme, without parents being able to select an a la carte education, it must also respect and take account of the parents' individual autonomy regarding the religious education of their children.

The conflict between religious freedom and the duties of employee athletes

The conflict that sometimes exists between the religious freedom of the athlete and players and their duties as employees, to the club that employs them, to ensure their optimal sporting performance,[46] and in order to be in the best possible condition. Imagine a situation in which an athlete, or player, who, in breach of his employment obligations, refuses to compete in a sport event, for religious reasons, because, according to their religion, the date of the event coincides with a day of rest, or a religious festival, for example, *Shabbat* and *Yom Kippur*, for Jews, or the classic example of the Muslim player, who plays while fasting during Ramadan, and is therefore not in peak condition.[47] Another example would be an Eastern Orthodox athlete, who strictly observes the days and periods, during which he is prohibited from eating meat, dairy products or eggs, and is therefore in breach of his obligations to his employer. Consider also, the case of a club with a sponsorship agreement with a betting company, and a player, who refuses to wear the club shirt because Islam prohibits the advertising of sport betting.[48]

These cases involve two separate aspects: firstly, the legal and/or contractual duty of athletes and players, to attend training, events and games, and their strict duty to ensure that they are in the best possible physical condition; secondly, athletes and players are not just athletes and players, they are also human beings, who want to live their religion according to their traditions, customs, rites and dictates, who must not be prejudiced because of their religious options. However, in the absence of appropriate contractual safeguards, it is quite possible that a club, or a sport company, could, as employers, commence disciplinary proceedings against a player for breach of their contractual and/or legal duties. Nevertheless, we consider that it is arguable that disciplinary penalties imposed (up to and including dismissal) could amount to violation of religious freedom,[49] particularly because religious freedom does not necessarily involve the absence of a certain level of sacrifice accepted by those who chose to join a particular religion, or to adopt a certain belief. Such discrimination would be contrary to European Union law: that is, Article 2(2) of Directive 2000/78/EC, which prohibits discrimination in employment on the grounds of religion, although it would be necessary to establish whether the reasons stated amount to a "*legitimate reason*". Furthermore, the UN Declaration on the Elimination of All Forms of Intolerance and Discrimination is based on Religion, or Belief (Resolution 36/55), Article 6(h) of which provides that "*the right to freedom of thought, consciousness, religion, or belief*" includes the freedom "to observe *days of rest, and to celebrate holidays and ceremonies in accordance with the precepts of one's religion, or belief*".

However, it is once again necessary to ensure the proportionality of the measures taken, or, as Rafael VALENCIA CANDALIJA proposes, to have recourse to a "*reasonable accommodation*", which seeks reasonable measures that ensure that certain personal characteristics, such as religion, do not obstruct the exercise of sport[50] as an occupation, particularly because recently "*religious freedom has been understood as a means to accommodate difference, in which the various societies should evolve towards a situation in which the various religious beliefs should be able to have the same opportunities for public manifestation* [together, we add, with other expressions of their religious choice], *particularly in employment.*"[51]

Conclusion

Religious freedom is not absolute and therefore admits exceptions, subject to the requirements of legality, legitimacy and proportionality. Accordingly, the recognised specificities of sport and the autonomy of sport organisations should always be considered, in each specific case, in order to determine whether a specific rule, or activity, within the context of sport, is, or is not, legal. This chapter shows that there are already sufficient cases in which human rights conflict that demonstrate that it is not easy to make a clear distinction between situations in which religious freedom is, or is not, violated, on a case-by-case basis. This is therefore a task for the Courts to which all sports actors, and all those who profess certain religions should be called, to state their reasons, which will be accepted, or not, according to the law.

Notes

1 Domingos PEREIRA DE SOUSA, *Introdução ao Direito*, Lisbon, Quid Juris Sociedade Editora, 2017, page 61.
2 L. BARBOSA RODRIGUES, *Introduction to Law: General, Internal, European Union and International*, 2nd Edition, Lisbon, Quid Iuris Sociedade Editora, 2015, page 43.
3 António CARLOS DOS SANTOS, André VENTURA and Elionora CARDOSO, "O Direito como Ordem Normativa e como Saber: Problemas Fundamentais", in *Introdução ao Direito*, Coord. Pedro TROVÃO DO ROSÁRIO, Anja BOTHE, António CARLOS DOS SANTOS, António PEDRO FERREIRA, Constança URBANO DE SOUSA, Jorge MORAIS CARVALHO and Stela BARBAS, Coimbra, Almedina, 2017, page 32.
4 Jorge MIRANDA and Rui MEDEIROS, C*onstituição Portuguesa Anotada,* Volume 1, 2nd Revised Edition, Lisbon, Universidade Católica Editora, 2017, page 658.
5 Cf. Article 18 of the Universal Declaration of Human Rights, 1948; Article 18(1) of the 1966 International Pact on Civil and Political Rights; Declaration on the elimination of all forms of intolerance and discrimination based on religion, or belief, proclaimed by the UN General Assembly in its resolution no. 36/55, of 25 November 1981; Article 8 of the African Charter on Human Rights and Peoples; Article 1.2 of the American Convention on Human Rights; Article 6(1) of the Asian Charter of Human Rights; Article 9 of the European Human Rights Convention; Article 10 of the European Union Charter of Fundamental Rights. It is therefore a universally recognised human right.
6 André ORTEGA COSTA, *Proteção da crítica religiosa: blasfémia e discurso anti – religioso na Convenção Europeia dos Direitos Humanos*, Lisbon, AAFDL Editora, 2020, pages 72–73.
7 Paulo FERREIRA DA CUNHA, D*ireitos Fundamentais: Fundamentos & Direitos Sociais,* Lisbon, Quid Juris Sociedade Editora, 2014, page 365.
8 Rabindranath V.A. CAPELO DE SOUSA, *O Direito Geral de Personalidade*, Coimbra Editora, 2011, page 272.

9 Guilhermo GARCIA GONZÁLEZ, "Relaciones laborales y libertad religiosa: su integración a partir de la jurisprudencia del Tribunal Europeo de Derechos Humanos", in *Religión y Derecho Internacional*, Dir. Miguel RODRÍGUEZ BLANCO and JUAN GONZÁLEZ AYESTA, UNIR, Granada, Editorial Comares, 2013, page 348.

10 Sara GUERREIRO, *As Fronteiras da Tolerância: Liberdade Religiosa e Proselitismo na Convenção Europeia dos Direitos do Homem*, Coimbra, Almedina, 2005, page 29.

11 Sara GUERREIRO, *As Fronteiras da Tolerância: Liberdade Religiosa e Proselitismo na Convenção Europeia dos Direitos do Homem*, Coimbra, Almedina, 2005, page 106.

12 Article 3 of the "Declaration on the elimination of all forms of intolerance and discrimination based on religion, or belief", proclaimed by the UN General Assembly in its resolution no. 36/55, of 25 November 1981. It is noteworthy that the 1945 version of the United Nations Charter includes non-discrimination on the grounds of religion, a provision also found in Article 2 of the UDHR and in Articles 2 and 26 of the International Pact on Civil and Political Rights. See Article 24(1) of the said Pact according to which the principle of non-discrimination for religious reasons applies to children.

13 Article 26(2) of the UDHR; Article 13(1) of the "International Pact on Economic, Social and Cultural Rights"; "Recommendation on education for international understanding, cooperation, and peace and education regarding Human Rights and fundamental freedoms", approved by the UN General Conference on 19 November 1974.

14 Article 29(1)(d) of the "Convention on the Rights of the Child".

15 Law no. 5/2007, of 16 January.

16 A document that Pope Francis referred to as the "*Encyclical on Sport*", in a recent interview with the Italian sports newspaper *Corriere dello Sport*, in the context of the "*globalisation of rights*" – see www.gazzetta.it/Altri-Mondi/02-01-2021/papa-francesco-sport-il-doping-annulla-dignita-3902144305876.shtml, accessed on 8 March 2021.

17 Article 4(1) of the Statutes.

18 Rule 16.1.3.

19 Rule 27.6.

20 Article 1.5.4.

21 Article 2(1) of the Statutes, under the heading "*Autonomy and operations*".

22 Article 2(1) of the Statutes, under the heading "*Independence and operations*".

23 Article 3, untitled.

24 Article 6(2) of the Statutes.

25 Free translation.

26 Cf. www.olympic.org/news/-freedom-of-expression-is-a-basic-human-right, accessed on 1 March 2021.

27 Rule 26.

28 "Rule 50 Guidelines Developed by the IOC Athletes' Commission", available at https://stillmedab.olympic.org/media/Document%20Library/OlympicOrg/News/2020/01/Rule-50-Guidelines-Tokyo-2020.pdf, accessed on 8 March 2021.

29 Rick SARRE, "Legislating for religious freedom in Australia: navigating the long and winding road", available at https://search.informit.org/doi/abs/10.3316/agispt.20200730034204, accessed on 8 March 2021.

30 Patrícia JERÓNIMO, "Símbolos e símbolos – o véu islâmico e o crucifixo na jurisprudência recente do Tribunal Europeu dos Direitos do Homem", in *Scentia Iuridica*, Tomo LIX, 2010, no. 323, page 505.

31 António MAGALHÃES, "O futebol debaixo do hijab", *Jornal Record*, 25 de Outubro de 2013, page 25.

32 Bruno PIRES and Otávio LOUSADA OLIVEIRA, "Judoca saudita proibida de usar véu durante a competição", *Diário de Notícias*, 27 July 2012, page 30.

33 Cécile MANTEL, "Signe religieux et pratique sportive: une nécessaire pédagogie", *Jurisport – La Revue Juridique et Économique du Sport*, no. 180, November 2017, page 14.

34 About this and other examples, in India and in the World, see Devisa AGARWAL, "*Does Right* to *Freedom Religion* extend to wearing *religious* headgear *during sporting* event, *Supreme Court asks Centre*", www.firstpost.com/india/does-right-to-freedom-extend-to-wearing-religious-headgear-during-sporting-event-supreme-asks-centre-4748901.html, accessed on 1 March 2021. *However, it is important to note that this evolution is* slow, even in the most universal sport event of all, that is, the Olympic Games: only in 1996 did the IOC authorise the entry of an athlete, wearing an Islamic veil that covered her body, into the Olympic Stadium; in 2000, on the occasion of the Sydney Olympic Games, the IOC suspended the Olympic Committee of Afghanistan because it required its female athletes to compete while wearing veils; at the 2012 London Olympic Games, Saudi judoka, Ali Shaherkani, paraded in a black *abaya*, and appeared on the tatami with her head covered.

35 Judgement *in Dogru v. France*, 4 December 2008, complaint no. 31645/04.

36 Judgement *in Osmanoglu and Kocabas v. France*, 10 January 2017, complaint no. 29086/12.

37 Article 3(1) of the ECHR.

38 In November 2019, the issue of the uniformity of equipment was on the agenda in Portugal in a case that was initially classed as religious discrimination. A 13-year-old Pakistani, Fatima Habid, a player at the Tavira Basketball Club, was prevented by the referee, from playing in a game because she refused to roll up the sleeves of the sweater she was wearing under her equipment. The player did not want to show her arms because this contradicted the family's religious tradition. The Portuguese Basketball Federation clarifies that there was an international regulatory requirement of the sport that was intended to standardise equipment and to ensure player safety, which had no religious or cultural connotations.

39 Jean-Pierre VIAL, "Liberté religieuse dans les associations sportives: une porte ouverte aux revendications identitaires", *Cahiers de Droit du Sport*, 2013, no. 33, page 33.

40 It is necessary to lobby the relevant national and international sports organisations for them to be more inclusive than exclusive, in particular

in the case of restrictive clothing regulations that could exclude Muslim women – "Women, Sport and the Challenge of Change" – Point 73 of the Conclusions of an International Conference held at the Grand Hotel, Brighton, United Kingdom, from 5 to 8 May 1994.

41 Vinicius M. CALIXTO, *Lex Sportiva e Direitos Humanos: Entrelaçamentos transconstitucionais e aprendizados recíprocos*, Editora D'Plácido, Belo Horizonte, 2017, pages 149–151.

42 "Women from all countries for the first time in History", *Diário Económico*, 27 June 2012, page 9.

43 This case is analysed by Jónatas Machado, "Liberdade de Pensamento, de pensamento, e religião", in *Comentário da Convenção Europeia dos Direitos Humanos e dos Protocolos Adicionais, Volume II*, Universidade Católica Editora, Lisbon, 2019, page 1665. This is the most complete and up-to-date article on the freedom in question, in terms of overall analysis.

44 Cf. Sami A. Aldeb ABU-SAHLIEH, "Limites du sport en droit musulman et arabe", in *Confluences Méditerranée* no. 50, Summer of 2004, pages 95 and 98.

45 These two judgements highlight the major significance of Physical Education in the curriculum, in the development and health of children, which overrides a right of enormous importance for a democratic society, such as religious freedom, cf. Konstantinos MARGARITIS, "Physical Education and Religious Freedom: The ECtHR Perspective", in *Law, Ethics and Integrity in the Sports Industry*, Greece, IGI Global, 2019, page 149.

46 Jonathan COLLINS, "Rugby union – is the practice and expression of religious beliefs compatible with professional playing obligations?", www.lawinsport.com/topics/item/rugby-union-is-the-practice-and-expression-of-religious-beliefs-compatible-with-professional-playing-obligations, accessed on 1 March 2021.

47 During the month of the Ramadan, which requires Muslims to fast (from dawn to sunset) and to refrain from sexual intercourse, many athletes refuse to compete during Ramadan. Others follow specific nutritional/dietary plans prescribed by physicians and nutritionists that enable them to dispense with food and drink during the day, without their performance being greatly affected. Others do not observe Ramadan and are subject to punishment.

48 Cf. R. Valencia CANDALIGA, "Está la religión en fuera de juego? Reflexiones relativas a la presencia de símbolos religiosos en el fútbol", in *Anuario de Derecho Eclesiástico del Estado*, XXIV (2018), pages 248–250.

49 Ian BLACKSHAW, *Sport and International Human Rights Law*, 45th Annual Study Session, Strasbourg, 7–25 July 2014, document provided by the author.

50 "El conflicto entre la religión y las obligaciones laborales en el fútbol: especial consideración sobre el descanso semanal y las festividades religiosas", *Revista Española de Derecho Deportivo*, no. 42 (2018–22), page 75.

51 Bruno Mestre, *Direito Antidiscriminação: Uma perspetiva europeia e comparada*, Porto, Vida Económica, 2020, page 118.

7 Why are protests by athletes and players regarding political, religious, racial or other causes restricted? Balancing the protection of human rights, the “Specificity of Sport” and other legal assets

Athletes in Olympic Games of Antiquity and rule compliance

Already, at the 776 BCE Olympic Games of Antiquity, the athletes were required, as a precondition of their participation in Games, to declare their express acceptance of the rules, that is, the athletes were required to make an express commitment to submit to the rules of the competition. This commitment took the form of an oath. Together with trainers, judges, relatives, friends, slave massagists and guards, athletes were required to make a solemn oath before the imposing statue of Zeus, “Sovereign of Olympus” and the “God of Oaths”, over the palpitating flesh of a pig offered as a burnt offering.

According to Pausanias, the oath had the following text: “*Beside this image it is the custom that athletes, their fathers, brothers, and their trainers, swear an oath upon the pieces of pig flesh, that in nothing will they sin against the Olympic Games. The athletes also took an additional oath that they had complied strictly with the training regulations for ten successive months. And that they would not have recourse to magical or unfair procedures. An oath was also taken by those who examine the boys, and horses involved in the races, that they would decide fairly, not take bribes, and that they would keep secret at matters they learned about candidates, whether admitted, or not.*”

The taking of the Oath was similar to a formal prior acceptance, or incorporation, procedure regarding not only sport-related issues but also ethical and deontological issues, by which sports actors submitted to the applicable rules, on pain of perjury. The function of oaths in sport and in other areas (e.g. in medicine, in the case of the famous Hippocratic oath) was to consolidate and strengthen contracts. Oaths were a more intensive and effective form of self-commitment, made in the presence of witnesses, and a guarantee, and a subjection to divine authority, in the event of breach.

DOI: 10.4324/9781003569749-9

When Pierre de Coubertin revived the Olympic Games of Antiquity, he instituted an oath in the Games of the Modern Era, in 1920, with the following text, which was read at the Opening Ceremony: *"We swear. We will take part in the Olympic Games in a spirit of chivalry, for the honour of our country and for the glory of sport."*

The European model of sport and the obligatory acceptance of a broad set of rules by athletes and players

The European model of sport is currently based on a pyramidal structure, with the International Olympic Committee (IOC) at the apex and the athletes at its base. Accordingly, when an athlete joins a club, they submit to its rules, and also to the rules to which the club is subject, that is, the rules governing the club's vertical relationship with the territorial association (if any) to which it belongs. The territorial association is, in turn, subject to the rules of the sport federation to which it belongs, and the federation is subject to the rules of the international sports federation. The international federation recognises continental confederations and requires them to comply with its bylaws, regulations and directives. The governance structure involves a cascade of rules, and a hierarchy that involves top-down subordination. As the athletes are at the base of the pyramid, it is easy to realise that the mere fact that they join a club means that they simultaneously submit to the rules issued by the national and international sports organisations that govern the sport, although they are unaware of this, in most cases.

The acceptance of multiple rules by athletes and players

Among other typical legal and contractual duties, athletes must undertake the sport activity for which they are engaged, and take part in training, training events and other preparatory sessions for competitions, with the determination and diligence corresponding to their mental, physical and technical preparedness, in accordance with the rules of the corresponding sport, and the instructions of the sports employer and to ensure that they are always in a physical condition that enables them to participate in the sport competition referred to in the contract.

(i) To these duties are added other, disparate, or linked, duties that arise also from Collective Bargaining Agreements and above all from internal regulations and codes of conduct, that is, the athlete's duty not to undertake any other physical activity, even during rest periods;
(ii) The duty of the athlete to go to bed early, and sometimes at a time predetermined by the employer, and, in some cases, subject to sleep-laboratory monitoring;
(iii) The duty of the athlete not to go out at night, even during rest periods, and particularly not to go to bars, discotheques and other public entertainment locations;

(iv) The duty of the athlete not to travel outside of a fixed kilometre radius, at night;
(v) The duty of the athlete not to consume alcoholic beverages and to keep their weight stable, even during holiday periods;
(vi) The duty of the athlete not to have sexual relations on the eve of games;
(vii) The duty of the athlete not to grant interviews, create personal blogs, post videos or photos, or write, on social networks, without the prior authorisation of the employer (club/sport company).

Athletes therefore have a large number of duties, which impress more because of their quality than because of their quantity, as they restrict fundamental rights and even human rights. Two examples of such duties are identified below before we seek to answer the question at the heart of this chapter. These two examples are the restriction of the human right to the inviolability, or protection, of private life, and the human right to access to due process.

Restriction of the right of athletes to privacy, and a private life, and their right to active rest

The duties of professional athletes, listed earlier, involve a clear restriction of the right of athletes to a private life, restrict their right to intimacy, even their right to active rest, and also amount, in practice, to the complete absence of working hours, even if their contract stipulates them. Professional athletes are subject to legal subordination, are required to obey orders and instructions at all times, and are likewise always at risk of violating their duties and of the consequent disciplinary proceedings, which can even result in their dismissal.

It should be borne in mind that the right to the inviolability, or protection, of private life, is a human right, under Article 12 of the Universal Declaration of Human Rights (UDHR), according to which *"No one shall be subjected to arbitrary interference with his privacy, family, home, or correspondence, nor to attacks upon his honour and reputation. Everyone has the right to the protection of the law against such interference or attacks."*[1] This right is the right of everyone to be protected from intrusion in their physical space, including the right to respect for their home, and the right of everyone to establish relations with their fellows. The personal private life of a person is inherently intimate, discrete, reserved, anonymous or even secret, unless, of course, the person in question wishes otherwise.

But . . . what about athletes? While the example of the concern regarding the privacy of athletes is a fact – for instance what is invoked by the IOC[2], it is nevertheless true that some of the examples mentioned earlier might not pass the proportionality test. Are they absolutely necessary for, or inherent in, the sport phenomenon? Is there no way, with a less restrictive impact on the athlete's private life, to achieve the same ends, that is, the maximisation of the athlete's performance, for the benefit of the sport and commercial interests of their employer (club/sport company) [not to mention the similar duties imposed by some national federations, on athletes, who are members of national teams, but who are no longer a party to an employment relationship]?

Moreover, the examples given earlier omit an area that is perhaps the most invasive of athlete's privacy, that is, anti-doping control, which pits the protection of two legal goods, that is, sport ethics and the protection of public health, against the athlete's human right to privacy. We shall now examine this issue in further detail, given its particular relevance.

As anti-doping control is implemented via the collection of blood, urine or sweat, it is an obvious intrusion into an athlete's private life,[3] and therefore a derogation of the principle of the inviolability of the human body. Nevertheless, and also given the nature of these controls, the majority view is that they can be justified objectively, for sport, moral, ethical, commercial, public health[4] and social reasons.

Furthermore, it should not be overlooked that anti-doping controls are not only conducted during competitions but between competitions, and that one of the "*Roles and Responsibilities of Athletes*", in Article 21.1.2 of the World Anti-Doping Code, is the duty to "*be available for sample collection at all times*". The underlying *reason* for this provision is evident from the Commentary on the Code: *"With due regard to a sport practitioner's human rights and privacy, legitimate anti-doping considerations sometimes require sample collection late at night or early in the morning. For example, it is known that some Sport Practitioners use low doses of EPO during these hours, which are undetectable in the morning.*" Despite the fact that we sympathise with this reasoning, and the fact that, in some countries, times are fixed at which controls are not permitted, it is nevertheless true that athletes are subject to control 24 hours a day, and even when at home,[5] or in a hotel room,[6] and at dawn, that is, at all times, which restricts their private lives. The argument that the right to nightly rest should limit the powers of the anti-doping authorities is of no avail, as the efficacy of the fight against doping trumps normal night-time rest and sleep.[7]

Indeed, the ECtHR[8] has validated this anti-doping control system. The ECtHR considered, notwithstanding the impact that the system had on the private lives of the applicants, that the important reasons of public interest inherent in the system, that is, the fight against doping and the growing risks of doping to the health of the sport community, prevail over the private interests invoked.

Similarly, and for the same reasons, the whereabouts athlete location scheme, under Article 5.6 of the World Anti-Doping Code, provides that "*Sport Practitioners who have been included in a Target Group by their International Federation and/or by their Anti-Doping Organization must provide information regarding their whereabouts.*" However, this system seems to amount to an excessive and disproportionate intrusion into the athlete's private life, by inserting work into the athlete's private life, in a continuous and perhaps insidious manner, as the athlete knows that they are subject to control at any time, even when on holiday. Moreover, when athletes are required to communicate how they occupy their days, not only in terms of their working lives but also in terms of their private lives, they are prevented from having a normal family life and have limited freedom of movement, as they are required to be at a predetermined place, at a predetermined time. This applies even during free time and family time, and involves a limitation of the athletes' freedom and dignity,[9] to the extent that athletes are virtually deprived of a private life.[10] However, here too the ECtHR has stated that this involves no unjustified violation of athletes' private lives.[11] In 2018, in proceedings brought by a number of athletes,[12] the ECtHR was required to balance conflicting interests and held that the whereabouts system was an objectively justified restriction, because it is a matter of public interest, and that the reduction or removal of relevant obligations of athletes would inevitably lead to increased doping and would be contrary to the consensus regarding the need for anti-doping controls outside of competitions.

Another sensitive issue, which is relevant to the matters considered in this chapter in the context of doping, is the so-called "*Athlete's Biological Passport*", which is the "*data collection and compilation programme and methods provided in the International Standard for Testing and Investigations in the International Standard for Laboratories*",[13] which is associated with the ADAMS Programme, and is defined as "*an Internet-based database tool that records, stores, shares and communicates data, which is designed to support interested parties and the WADA in the conduct of their anti-doping activities, in accordance with data protection legislation*".[14] If we consider that the traceability of athletes' performances during their careers requires that a great volume of athletes' biological data is made available to sport federations, it is appropriate to consider whether this requirement is potentially excessive when balanced against athletes' private lives, particularly as they are not allowed a free choice of their doctor, and their medical confidentiality and the protection of their medical data is prejudiced.

It is also necessary not to overlook the fact that an athlete's health is part of their private life and is protected as such.[15] A person's health is an important part of their private life, which involves "*sensitive data*" within the meaning of the European Union's General Data Protection Regulation (GDPR),[16] so the confidentiality of such data is a relevant issue. However, anti-doping involves the collection and storage of data that may not be used immediately, not to mention the fact that it involves a publication/dissemination of data that is a violation of the protected status of personal information and an intrusion into the private lives of the athletes in question. The response of the World Anti-Doping Agency to these questions is that "*it seeks to protect the private life of the sportsperson as much as possible, and principally by protecting the data collected in the context of anti-doping controls, and the ADAMS programme, in accordance with international personal data protection standards, in order to ensure that its agents in the fight against doping apply a minimum level of protection to the personal data collected in the fight against doping.*"[17]

Limitation of access to the courts/fair and equitable process for athletes

Another example of the circumstances in which athletes are vulnerable to the extent that they are deprived of their human rights, merely because they are athletes, via their acceptance of a series of legal impositions, is the issue of access to the courts and athletes' right to due process.

It is important, by way of an introduction, to be aware that the UDHR guarantees everyone access to a competent national jurisdiction in order to challenge *"acts violating the fundamental rights granted him by the constitution or by law"*[18] and enshrines the right of all persons to *"a fair and public hearing by an independent and impartial tribunal, in the determination of his rights and obligations and of any criminal charge against him" "in full equality"*.[19] Article 6 of the European Convention on Human Rights (ECHR) provides that *"In the determination of his civil rights and obligations or of any criminal charge against him, everyone is entitled to a fair and public hearing within a reasonable time by an independent and impartial tribunal established by law. Judgment shall be pronounced publicly but the press and public may be excluded."*[20]

Essentially, the aim is to ensure the right of access to justice, the right to commence and sue out proceedings before an independent/impartial court, including an effective right of appeal, and due process, in which each party has a reasonable opportunity to defend their interests in a position that is not inferior to the other party, including adversarial procedure, on equal terms.

However, here too, athletes have been deprived of a human right, to the extent that sport organisations, that is, international sports federations, tend to prohibit members, athletes, trainers, leaders, clubs, etc., either entirely or with a few minor exceptions, from accessing ordinary courts of law, and often punish those who breach this prohibition, severely, with disciplinary penalties that may even result in a demotion/disqualification/relegation. International sports federations, and also national federations, because of the cascade and hierarchy of rules set out earlier, include these prohibitions and penalties in their statutes and regulations, together with provisions that limit access to justice to the mechanisms of "sport justice" within the federation judicial structure (disciplinary committees, Councils of justice, or appeal, boards of ethics, and other bodies with other names) and arbitration proceedings (arbitration committees and tribunals). It is therefore generally necessary for disputes to be decided and resolved within a limited judicial/arbitration framework, without access to the state judicial system. Consequently, as athletes are required to comply with the said statutes and regulations, they thereby consequently and automatically waive recourse to the ordinary courts, which is a human right.

Recently, in the famous *Mutu/Pechstein* Case,[21] the ECtHR considered an arbitration clause in the regulations of an international sports federation, that is, the ISU. The ECtHR held that despite the fact that the clause had not been imposed by law, but by an ISU regulation, the acceptance of the jurisdiction of CAS by the complainant amounted to *forced arbitration* as interpreted by the case law of the ECtHR. However, CAS considered that there is valid justification for this: namely the interest in allowing disputes in professional sport, particularly those with an international dimension, to be decided by a specialist and uniform jurisdiction, such as CAS, which operates as a single international court that resolves disputes that are directly, or indirectly, related to sport, quickly and economically. CAS further argued that the Swiss Federal Court has the power to annul CAS judgements, if the basic procedural guarantees are not complied with, which ensures compliance with Article 6 of the ECHR. It should also be noted that ECtHR stated in its judgement that the CAS system is sufficiently independent and impartial, that is, in terms of the procedures for the selection and appointment of arbitrators and also, here upholding the case argued by the applicant, that the absence of a public hearing in "*less serious*" cases may not be incompatible with Article 6(1) of the ECHR, but is incompatible with Article 6(1), in civil cases, in which the public nature of the hearing is fundamental and important.[22]

In short, once again, the specificities and needs of sport and sport organisations cause athletes to lose out, because they are the weakest link. Nevertheless, it is noteworthy that the ECtHR held, similarly, for example, in doping cases, that the measures were proportionate and therefore valid, and that the fact that sport organisations restrict rights does not necessarily mean that they do so with intent to prejudice athletes. However, and in the defence of sport organisations that wish to ensure due process, it is noted, for example, that the World Anti-Doping Agency provides as follows in Article 8.1 of the World Anti-Doping Code, under the heading "*Fair hearing*": *"For any Person who is asserted to have committed an anti-doping rule violation, the Anti-Doping Organization with responsibility for Results Management shall provide, at a minimum, a fair hearing within a reasonable time by a fair, impartial and Operationally Independent hearing panel.*" Any doubts regarding this matter are assuaged by the following Commentary on Article 8.1: "*These principles are also found in Article 6.1 of the Convention for the Protection of Human Rights and Fundamental Freedoms and are principles generally accepted in international law.*"

Restriction of the freedom of expression and opinion of athletes

The logic underlying the restrictions of the two human rights identified earlier helps us to answer the question posed at the beginning of this chapter and refers us to another human right, that is, the right of freedom of expression and opinion.

According to Article 19 of the UDHR, *"Everyone has the right to freedom of opinion and expression; this right includes freedom to hold opinions without interference and to seek, receive and impart information and ideas through any media and regardless of frontiers."*[23] Moreover, Article 10(1) of ECHR provides that *"This right shall include freedom to hold opinions and to receive and impart information and ideas without interference by public authority and regardless of frontiers"*, while Article 10(2) provides that *"The exercise of these freedoms, since it carries with it duties and responsibilities, may be subject to such formalities, conditions, restrictions or penalties as are prescribed by law and are necessary in a democratic society, in the interests of national security, territorial integrity or public safety, for the prevention of disorder or crime, for the protection of health or morals, for the protection of the reputation or rights of others, for preventing the disclosure of information received in confidence, or for maintaining the authority and impartiality of the judiciary."*

These provisions mean that it is a matter of general agreement that when there is censorship in a country that hosts a certain sport event, the media become an instrument of propaganda, which is completely alien to the idea of the promotion of human rights in sport.[24] This is also true when foreign journalists, who are accredited to cover that event, and seek to disseminate information that the said countries do not want to be made public, are the victims of threats, intimidation or imprisonment. It is precisely under the said legal framework that it is sought to ensure, by law or contract, that when an organiser of sport competition makes an exclusive contract with a television station for the broadcast of the events in that competition, that the said exclusive right respects the right of journalists to inform the public (which also involves freedom of the press and the right to information), which is generally achieved via the sublicensing of the rights at the market price, and/or by the right to broadcast extracts/short summaries of the event.

However, the conciliation of freedom of expression and opinion, on the one hand, and some of the specificities of the sport, on the other hand, is less evident. The following are some examples.

Firstly, and as indicated earlier, the internal regulations of some clubs prohibit players from granting interviews, and from speaking publicly. This control of the freedom of expression of sportspersons appears to amount to an "*excessive obligation of loyalty to the club*",[25] but, at the same time, and in defence of the employer, it be viewed as absolutely necessary in order to safeguard the club's image, for the stability of the group and to protect certain team secrets.

Moreover, it is also difficult to reconcile freedom of expression with sport ethics, and there are already relevant judicial decisions that provide clues in that regard. The ECtHR has already decided[26] that doping in "*professional sport*", that is, in cycling, involves a very important public interest debate, and therefore that articles/reports in newspapers and magazines on the subject respond to the growing and legitimate demand of the public to have information on doping practices in sport, particularly in cycling. This can mean that judicial authorities search the premises/headquarters of newspapers and magazines, in this case, the newsroom of the French publications, *L'Équipe* and *Le Point*, even if this could jeopardise the rights of journalists. Likewise, CAS had held[27] that *"the exposing of illegal practices linked to major sporting events, such as corruption, doping, or game fixing, is a matter of public interest. Moreover, and in the light of the case law of the European Court of Human Rights, it is not clear that the conduct of the journalists, even if is malicious, is illegal.*" It is therefore important to realise that the public interest, associated with the protection of sport ethics, can justify acts that would otherwise be a violation of freedom of expression, and of opinion.

It can be seen from these cases that athletes are not the only ones, who have to give way to values such as sport ethics, which are viewed as superior. However, the truth is that it is athletes who face most barriers because they are subject to the cascade of rules within the pyramidal structure into which they are inserted.

Sport organisations enact rules that limit the right of athletes to adopt political, religious, racial or other positions,[28] and Rule 50 of the Olympic Charter is the most evident case of this. This rule provides that *"No kind of demonstration or political, religious or racial propaganda is permitted in any Olympic sites, venues, or other areas.*"[29] However, although the IOC issued a statement titled *"Freedom of expression: a basic human right*",[30] during the presidency of Jacques Rogge, it is also true that the IOC also stated that the Games are not the place where any political or religious positions should be expressed by athletes, as more than 200 countries and territories are represented at the Olympic Games, many of which are in conflict. The IOC called for "*common sense*" in the application of this rule, and stated that it was protecting the right of athletes not to state an opinion, to which they are also entitled.

In order to pursue its aim to exclude politics from the Olympic Games, the IOC states in the Olympic Charter the view that sport must be neutral, both in Fundamental Principle 5, which recognises that the sport that occurs in society and in sport organisations, within the Olympic Movement, "*must apply political neutrality*", and in Rule 2(5), which states that the mission of the IOC is "*to maintain and promote the political neutrality*" of the Olympic Movement.

The IOC also seeks to ensure "*internally*", that is, within the sport event, that there are no reasons why athletes could suffer discrimination, by providing in Fundamental Principle no. 6 that there shall be no discrimination against athletes on political or religious grounds, in the exercise of their rights and freedoms.

In any event, it is at least necessary to query the solution in Rule 50, as the paradigm of many other rules regarding athletes' freedom of expression and opinion.

It is our opinion that the expression of an opinion should not be confused with propaganda or demonstrations. We agree with the IOC that sport events should not be used by athletes to conduct a campaign or propagandise in favour of a certain political regime, or religion, either by supporting it or by criticising other regimes or religions. A sport event, a sport infrastructure, is not the proper place for such things.

We are not unaware that the IOC has already made it clear that athletes can express themselves freely at press conferences and on the various media platforms, as these are not part of the Olympic infrastructure,[31] that is, they are outwith the competitive sport arena.

Likewise, we understand the argument that measures, including the adoption of rules, must be taken to curb athletes, who want to "*bring politics into the stadium*".[32] We consider that whatever the political, religious, war-related, or other nature of the protest, that the rules make sense if the underlying reason for them is the specificity of sport and the need to limit sport events to that specificity.[33] However, there is no such justification, if the underlying reason for the rules is the protection of public order and not the preservation of the specificity of sport, athlete protests are not a threat to public order.

We are however also sensitive to the material and commercial concerns of the IOC and organisers of other sport mega-events, that is, their desire to combat ambush marketing, in order to protect the commercial value of events. This involves the restriction of the freedom of expression of companies that are not business partners of the Olympic Games, and of the athletes who compete in the Games, who are required to surgically remove, or at least cover, tattoos that contain the Olympic rings.[34] The IOC can also claim that although the Olympic rings are "*Olympic Property*", to which the IOC is exclusively entitled, under Rule 8 et seq. of the Olympic Charter. Indeed, the ECtHR has held that Article 1 of Protocol 1 of the ECHR, regarding the protection of property, also applies to intellectual property,[35] because the said protocol makes no distinction based on the tangible, or intangible, nature of assets. Consequently, it seems to be the position that the Olympic symbols are assets, within the meaning of the ECHR, and are therefore protected under the Convention.[36]

Nevertheless, and notwithstanding our preceding observations, the truth is that athletes are still unable to express their political, religious or other convictions freely at key moments, when the eyes of the world are on them, that is, when they are competing, have just competed, or are on the podium. Once again, athletes are compelled to defer. For example, in the cases already outlined earlier, in which sport organisations, of which the IOC is a classic example,[37] adopt rules that prohibit or restrict Internet and social media communication, by sport actors, particularly athletes, some authors, such as Catherine FRUTEAU,[38] highlight the following paradox: although the Olympic Movement always poses as a guarantor of fundamental rights, it sometimes betrays the ideas of Pierre de Coubertin, and fails to protect fundamental rights, because of its material interests. To which we add that the athlete is the loser.

Conclusion

We shall now attempt to answer the question posed at the beginning of this chapter. We consider that the frequently restrictive, prohibitive, limitative and controlling framework that is generally imposed on athletes, for example, the restrictions of their right to a private life, or of access to public courts in order to defend their rights, is also the reason for the restriction of the right of athletes to protest in support of political, religious, racial, war-related or other causes.

However, this is inevitable, in the governance of sport as we know it. This is not a recent situation. Even in the days of the Oath in the Olympic Games of Antiquity, which Pierre de Coubertin included in the Olympic Games of the Modern Era, the European model of sport model was structured in a way that when an athlete, who is at the base of the pyramid, joins a club, he is automatically subject to a vast and complex group of rules not only of the club but also of all the organisations that rank above within the pyramid.

As we have seen earlier, it is necessary to restrict human rights, primarily in the name of the "specificity of sport", on the one hand, and the vital struggle for sport ethics, on the other, and sometimes in an objectively justified manner. Indeed, the ECtHR has held in several cases that rules of sports organisation that limit athletes' human rights are valid, provided that the principle of proportionality is respected. The restriction of athletes' human rights is also justified for reasons of public health, and even by the material/commercial concerns of event organisers, or their concern to ensure the political and religious neutrality of the event.

However, we consider that it is necessary not to forget, as the World Players Association states, that *"Players are people first and athletes second . . . Players therefore sit at the intersection between sport and human rights."*[39] The balancing of the various values in play in this intersection requires great care and consideration. As J.P. Margúenaud states, in the same line of thought, "*sport organisations, supported by the LexSportiva, must not give way to the temptation to operate in a closed loop, and avoid the influence of human rights, as if sportspersons, by being sportspersons, cease to be human beings first and foremost.*"[40] On the other hand, we cannot overlook the fact that sport is specific and requires a modulated application of the rules, which cannot be applied indiscriminately, or blindly, as if sport was a sector like any other.

Notes

1 Cf. also Article 17 of the ICCP; Article 7 of the EU Charter of Fundamental Rights; Article IX of the American Declaration of the Rights and Duties of Man.

2 Kéba MBAYE, "Droits de l'Homme et Olympisme", in *Karel Vasak Amicorum Liber – Les Droits de l'Homme à l'aube du XXIe Siécle*, Bruyllant, Brussels, 1999, page 1075.

3 George PETRITSCH, "WADA's 'whereabouts system' – Athlete's price to pay? An abstract of the latest developments", *Pandektis – International Sports Law Review*, 8, Issues 1–2 (2009), page 112.
4 Authors such as Evan RASCHEL consider that public health is not the real foundation of the anti-doping struggle and that *fair play* is an ethical and moral rule, and, as such, cannot be the source of restrictions that violate the rights and freedoms of persons presumed to be innocent – cf. "Le dopage face à la Convention européenne de sauveguarde des droits de l'Homme", *Cahiers de Droit du Sport*, 2013, no. 84.
5 The Human Rights Committee considers that a person's home is the place where they reside or the place where they habitually perform their occupation – cf. the judgement in *Niemietz v. Germany*, of 16 December 1992.
6 According to the case law of the ECtHR, and in light of the current living conditions, the concept of domicile should include a hotel room, particularly in cases where athletes spend the night at a hotel, during training events – see Philippe FRUMER, "La vie privée des sportifs professionnels sous la surveillance. Le Code Mondial Antidopage à l'épreuve de la Convention Européenne des Droits de L´Homme", in *Le nouveau code mondial antidopage: Évolution et perspectives*, Dir. Cécile CHAUSSARD and THIÉRRYCHIRON, Année 2016, Volume 45, Paris, Lexis Nexis, 58.
7 Cf. Ramón TÉROL GOMEZ, "El derecho al descanso nocturno del deportista como límite a la potestad de las autoridades competentes para la realización de controles de dopaje en España", *Dopaje, Intimidad y Datos Personales: Especial referencia a los aspectos penales y político-criminales*, Madrid, Iustel, 2010, pages. 141 et seq.
8 Cf. judgement *in Fédération Nationale des Syndicats Sportifs (FNASS) and others v. France*, 48151/11 and 77769/13.
9 Delphine GARDES and Lionel MINIATO, "Le sportif professionnel exerce-t-il un 'travail décent'?", in *Éthique en matiére sportive*, Dir. Delphines GARDES and Lionel MINIATO, Presses de l' Úniversité Toulouse 1 Capitole, 2016, pages 45 and 46.
10 Adam PENDLEBURY and John McGARRY, "Location, Location, Location: The Whereabouts Rule and the Right to Privacy", *The Cambrian Law Review*, 40 (2009), page 71.
11 *Longo and Cipreeli v. France*, Case 77769 (13).
12 *Cf. Fédération Nationale des Syndicats Sportifs (FNASS) and others v. França*, 48151/11 and 77769/13.
13 Annex 1 of the WAC, "*Definitions*".
14 Anexo 1 of the WAC, "*Definitions*".
15 Tatiana VASSINE, "Eclaircissements sur l'obligation de loyauté du sportif professionnel", *Cahiers de Droit du Sport*, 1008, np. 13, page 132.
16 Regulation (EU) No 679/2016, of 27 April.
17 "A Dopagem no Desporto", in *Direitos Humanos e Ética no desporto*, Coord. Jónatas E.M. MACHADO, Coimbra, Coimbra Editora, 2015, page 343.
18 Article 8.
19 Article 10.
20 Article 14 of the ICCPR; Article 47 of the EU Charter of Fundamental Rights; Articles 7 and 16 of the African Charter of Human and Peoples'

Rights; Article XVIII of the American Declaration of the Rights and Duties of Man.

21 *Mutu and Pechstein v. Suiça*, Complaints nos. 40575/10 and 674/10, Judgement of 2 October 2018 (final on 4 February 2019).

22 Patricia GALÀN and Juan Prieto HUANG, "Sobre la sentencia del TEDH en los casos Mutu y Penchestein", https://iusport.com/art/72199/sobre-la-sentencia-del-tedh-en-los-casos-mutu-y-penchestein.

23 Cf. Article 19 of the ICCPR; Article 11 of the EU Charter of Fundamental Rights; Article 9 of the African Charter of Human and Peoples' Rights; Article IV of the American Declaration of the Rights and Duties of Man.

24 Cf. *Final Report of the Human Rights Council Advisory Committee on the possibilities of using sport and the Olympic ideal to promote human rights for all and to strengthen universal respect for them*, 17 Agosto de 2015, page 46.

25 Baptiste FAUCHER, *La santé du sportif professionnel salarié*, Centre de Droit et Économie du Sport Aix-Marseille, Presses Universitaires d'Aix-Marseille, 2015, page 197.

26 *Judgment in Ressiot and other v. France*, 28 June 2012, Cases 15054/07 and 15066/07.

27 CAS 2011/A/2433 *Amadou Diakite v. FIFA*, judgement of 8 March 2012, Sumar, paragraph 3, free translation.

28 Inversely, the American footballer Clin Kaepernick, who in 2016 remained seated during the anthem of the United States of America, and stated that he would not stand because his country oppresses black people, was not punished, because of the lack of any applicable legal provision. There was no penalty, that is, employment penalty, because the matter was not dealt with in the Collective Bargaining Contract or in the NFL Rulebook. Cf. Johan LINDHOLM, "From Carlos to Kaepernick and beyond: athlete's right to freedom of expression, disposable", https://link.springer.com/article/10.1007/s40318-017-0117-4

29 Free translation.

30 www.olympic.org/news/-freedom-of-expression-is-a-basic-human-right, accessed on 1 March 2021.

31 "Rule 50 Guidelines Developed by the IOC Athletes' Commission", available at https://stillmedab.olympic.org/media/Document%20Library/OlympicOrg/News/2020/01/Rule-50-Guidelines-Tokyo-2020.pdf, accessed on 8 March 2021.

32 Richard GIULIANOTTI, "Human Rights, Globalization and Sentimental Education: The Case of Sport", in *Sport, Civil Liberties and Human Rights*, Ed. Richard GIULIANOTI and David McCARDLE, New York, Routledge, 2006, page 68, free translation.

33 José LUIS PÉREZ TRIVINO, "Freedom of Expression and Political Opinions in Sport Stadiums", available at www.researchgate.net/publication/330746094_Freedom_of_Expression_and_Political_Opinions_in_Sport_Stadiums_Proceedings_of_the_2016_Meeting_of_the_International_Association_for_the_Philosophy_of_Sport_at_the_International_Olympic_Academy.

34 Ian BLACKSHAW, *Sport and International Human Rights Law*, 45th Annual Study Session, Strasbourg, 7–25 July 2014, document provided by the author.

35 Judgement of 11 January 2007, *Anheuser-Busch Inc v. Portugal*, Case 73049/01.
36 Emilie TERRIER, "La protection nationale des signes olympiques confrontée à la liberté d'expression", *Cahiers de Droit du Sport*, n.º 31 (2013), page 143.
37 "Les droits fondamentaux au sein du Mouvement Olympique", *Droit & Olympisme: Contribution à l'étude juridique d'un phénomène transnational*, Dir. Mathieu MAISONNEUVE, Presses Universitaires d'Aix-Marseille, 2015, page 60.
38 Cf., inter alia, *IOC Social Media Blogging, and Internet Guidelines for participants and other accredited persons at the London 2012 Olympic Games* e *IOC Social and Digital Media Guidelines for persons accredited to the XXII Olympic Winter Games PyeongChang 2018*.
39 Introduction to the *World Player Rights Policy*.
40 Jean-Pierre MARGUÉNAUD, *Droits de l'Homme, Dictionnaire Juridique du Sport*, Dalloz, 2013, page 149.

Index

For Product Safety Concerns and Information please contact our EU representative GPSR@taylorandfrancis.com
Taylor & Francis Verlag GmbH, Kaufingerstraße 24, 80331 München, Germany

www.ingramcontent.com/pod-product-compliance
Lightning Source LLC
LaVergne TN
LVHW010840120826
845149LV00017B/3320

* 9 7 8 1 0 3 2 9 4 2 6 1 2 *